Anger and Assertiveness
in Pastoral Care

David W. Augsburger

Fortress Press Philadelphia

Creative Pastoral Care and Counseling Series
Editor: Howard J. Clinebell, Jr.
Associate Editor: Howard W. Stone

The Care and Counseling of Youth in the Church by Paul B. Irwin
*Growth Counseling for Marriage Enrichment: Pre-Marriage and
the Early Years* by Howard J. Clinebell, Jr.
Crisis Counseling
by Howard W. Stone
Pastoral Care and Counseling in Grief and Separation
by Wayne E. Oates
Counseling for Liberation by Charlotte Holt Clinebell
Growth Counseling for Mid-Years Couples
by Howard J. Clinebell, Jr.
Theology and Pastoral Care by John B. Cobb, Jr.
Pastor and Parish—A Systems Approach by E. Mansell Pattison
Pastoral Care with Handicapped Persons by Lowell G. Colston
The Care and Counseling of the Aging by William M. Clements
Anger and Assertiveness in Pastoral Care by David W. Augsburger

Library of Congress Cataloging in Publication Data

Augsburger, David W
    Anger and assertiveness in pastoral care.

    (Creative pastoral care and counseling series)
    Bibliography: p.
    1. Pastoral counseling.   2. Pastoral psychology.
    3. Anger.   4. Aggressiveness (Psychology)   I. Title.
    BV4012.2.A87   253   78-14660
    ISBN 0-8006-0562-4

Second printing 1982

9720F82   Printed in the United States of America   1-562

Contents

65328

Series Foreword

Let me share with you some of the hopes that are in the minds of those of us who helped to develop this series—hopes that relate directly to you as the reader. It is our desire and expectation that these books will be of help to you in developing better working tools as a minister-counselor. We hope that they will do this by encouraging your own creativity in developing more effective methods and programs for helping people live life more fully. It is our intention in this series to affirm the many things you have going for you as a minister in helping troubled persons—the many assets and resources from your religious heritage, your role as the leader of a congregation, and your unique relationship to individuals and families throughout the life cycle. We hope to help you reaffirm *the power of the pastoral* by the use of fresh models and methods in your ministry.

The aim of the series is not to be comprehensive with respect to topics but rather to bring innovative approaches to some major types of counseling. Although the books are practice-oriented, they also provide a solid foundation of theological insights. They are written primarily for ministers (and those preparing for the ministry) but we hope that they will also prove useful to other counselors who are interested in the crucial role of spiritual and value issues in all helping relationships. In addition we hope that the series will be useful in seminary courses, clergy support groups, continuing education workshops, and lay befriender training.

This is a period of rich new developments in counseling and psychotherapy. The time is ripe for a flowering of creative methods and insights in pastoral care and counseling. Our expectation is that this series will stimulate grass-roots creativity as innovative methods and programs come alive for you. Some of the major thrusts that will be discussed in this series include a new awareness of the unique contributions of the theologically trained counselor, the liberating power of the human potentials orientation, and appreciation of the pastoral care function of the ministering congregation, the importance of humanizing systems and institutions as well as close relationships, the importance of pastoral *care* (and not just counseling), the many opportunities for caring ministries throughout the life cycle, the deep changes in male-female relationships, and the new psychotherapies such as Gestalt therapy, Transactional Analysis, educative counseling, and crisis methods. Our hope is that this series will enhance your resources for your ministry to persons by opening doorways to understanding of these creative thrusts in pastoral care and counseling.

This volume by David Augsburger explores a problem which has received scant attention in the pastoral care literature—how anger and aggression can be handled constructively. To get a feel for the potential usefulness of this book, think of the ways in which distorted Christian theology has contributed to the destructive handling of anger. Recall those congregations you have known where an epidemic of mishandled anger infected, and in some cases destroyed, the vitality of Christian community. Reflect briefly on how often unfaced or misdirected anger, turned on oneself or others destructively, is at the heart of problems which bring people to pastoral counselors. Or, to come close to home, perhaps be aware of how anger, toward us or from us as ministers, can diminish our effectiveness as facilitators of healing and growth.

The aim of this book is to help us think more clearly, feel more openly, and act more effectively in anger-fraught relationships. The author begins the book at a most helpful place, with a discussion of how we as ministers deal with our own anger. As a person with years of experience in mishandling mine, I found his illuminating description of the dynamics of such mishandling uncomfortably familiar. The basic pattern is one of alternating between the accumulation of anger through being a "nice guy" and the eventual explosion of this pent-up energy in hurting aggression. I have a hunch that this pattern will be familiar to some other pastors who read the book.

Fortunately the book moves beyond the two unproductive extremes of repression and aggression to a middle way of creative assertion. The discussion moves far beyond the limited prescriptions of "express your anger" and "assert your rights," so popular in contemporary thought, to describe how anger can be channeled in ways that can be both wholeness-creating for individuals and community-building for congregations. The author builds on Paul Tillich's thought that loveless power violates, powerless love abdicates, but power and love in balance create both justice and community. He shows how balancing affirmation and assertion, caring and confrontation, can help strengthen relationships and bring more openness, healing, and trust to a community. He gives practical methods by which pastors can help their people learn constructive assertiveness and suggests how congregations can gain release from being anger-accumulating, potentially explosive communities. Particularly useful are the suggestions of concrete steps to use in pastoral counseling to facilitate growth in handling anger more constructively.

Most approaches to psychotherapy offer some insights which help us in understanding the basic human energy which produces anger and aggressiveness. But the three approaches upon which this volume draws—Gestalt-existentialist, psychoanalytic, and learning theory therapies—seem particularly rich in illuminating insights and in methods of dealing with this vital human energy in growthful ways.

David Augsburger teaches pastoral care and counseling at Associated Mennonite Biblical Seminaries in Elkhart, Indiana. Before coming to his present job, he taught at Northern Baptist Theological Seminary. Before that he was a radio and television spokesperson for the three Mennonite denominations. I know David to be a warmhearted, effective pastor and counselor, a creative teacher, and a writer of numerous books in the fields of relationships, communication, and conflict resolution. This book grows out of his continuing interest in methods of reconciliation through conflict reeducation in churches. I predict that it will prove to be a significant and useful volume for pastors, members of church staffs, and lay church leaders. It will be helpful to anyone who wants to learn how to transform the life energy which is wasted in unconstructive anger and conflict into the energy of growth-in-community.

HOWARD J. CLINEBELL, JR.

Preface

I am an angry person.

Having written this opening line and then crossed it out twice for fear of being misunderstood, I recognize once again how automatic my denial of my own anger can be. But the fact is that I *am* an angry person. I am an angry minister, pastoral counselor, husband, and father. More and more, though, I am coming to see and experience that my anger is expressive of my creative life energies. Increasingly I feel free to be angry. And as I am increasingly able—at least much of the time—to be angry in useful and uniting ways, I find that the important people in my life are also increasingly appreciative of the resultant arousal and excitement, their own as well as mine. And when I fail to work out my anger . . . well, we are learning from that too.

I am an assertive person.

Having grown up as a pleaser, a placater, a knee-jerk nice guy, I entered the ministry full of messiah needs. "They have to appreciate me," I thought, "especially since I've been so helpful to them." But they didn't. Once their pain has subsided, or their dependency is outgrown or outmaneuvered, people don't any longer care much for the nice-guy savior and helper. My learning has been slow in this respect, but more and more I am learning the integrity, freedom, and mutuality of clearly assertive and openly affirmative living.

I am an affirmative person.

People are worthful. They are irreducibly valuable. Nothing can diminish their essential worth as created and potentially creative beings. Increasingly as I come to prize the worth of persons, I am excited by the uniting, bonding, community-building power of trust, the deep trust that can come with deep encounter and contact with others. Such contact must value anger. Contact—or trust—that bypasses anger is only partial, a touch-and-go contact with only the positive side of persons. It misses the power inherent also in the negative side.

I am an angry, assertive, and affirmative person—and that no longer frightens me, even in my ministerial roles. I am an angry pastor. And I am discovering that anger that is expressed in assertive and affirmative ways can be powerful and healing. Channeling it can play a rich and important part in the pastoral care of whole persons.

Three major streams of psychotherapy have contributed to the approach used in this book. The psychoanalytic model is appreciated for its illumination of the hidden and unconscious dynamics of denial and distortion by which we recirculate anger into other emotional and physical responses. The Gestalt-existential model is applied to the experiencing and expressing of anger in responsible humanity that prizes and presses forward with the whole self. The behavioral and social learning models of assertive and affirmative behavior are utilized for examining the old behaviors and learning/reinforcing the new.

The book turns away from a ventilationist therapy that recommends the explosive behavior we hope eventually to eliminate. It turns instead toward an assertive-affirmative expression of anger which models and reinforces responses that can create solidarity with others. This is not to deny the value of an uncensored expression of rage; in therapy such an approach can often bring the unaware to awareness. It is to assert that as a temporary means toward anger management catharsis has only limited effectiveness. After ten years of research Leonard Berkowitz of the University of Wisconsin concludes: "The evidence dictates now that it is unintelligent to encourage persons to be aggressive, even if, with the best of intentions, we want to limit such behavior to the confines of psychotherapy."*

When pastoral counseling addresses itself to anger and offers new styles of awareness, focusing, channeling, and expression, people can creatively disconnect from the old ways of emotional flooding whereby they are often overwhelmed in instant anger and shocked by their own outbursts. The goal of both the Gestalt and behavioral approaches is to disconnect emotion from volition so that the two are free to check and balance each other. For some persons, this disconnecting may momentarily seem to reinforce old patterns of denial rather than foster the new freedom of creative detachment. But denying and disconnecting are not the same:

When my breath is coming in short spurts, when my voice is flat with overcontrol or metallic in tone, when my stomach is in knots and I'm concealing, suppressing, or civilizing my feelings, that is denial. It is neither a healthy response to me nor a healthful reaction to you. If I am not even aware that any or all of the above are happening within me, then ventilating and pillow pounding in private may be a channel for self-discovery.

On the other hand, when I am aware of your anger at me and can identify my demands, experience them with some arousal, and then either put them into words now, hold them for later, or let go of them as unimportant, that is disconnecting. To be able to bring angry, obsessive thoughts from their exaggerated enlargement back into proper size is to disconnect emotion from volition and to experience both in mind-body wholeness.

In the chapters which follow, you will perhaps make some new connections, and even some disconnections. As insight increases, try also to detach volition from emotion. Claim a little more freedom to be angry, to be assertive, to be affirmative. Claim the freedom to be who you truly are in a whole and healthful way. It can enhance the excitement and effectiveness of ministry.

1. The Angry Pastor—Appreciating Aliveness

Ordained. It makes a difference.

No anger here. (God forbid. God's people forbid.)

No malicious gossip. (Although sharing a spicy prayer request may release a little ministerial tension.)

No resentment. (Although holding a "concern" against a sister or brother may balance a pastor's internal ledger of grievances.)

No temper. (Although intense vocal expression of righteous indignation may reduce the clergy's consternation.)

No irritability. (Although being a bit short in speech when feeling "burdened with the care of souls" may restore serenity.)

No hostile rejection. (Although encouraging a problem-maker to consider another church home may pass as peacemaking.)

No wrath or rage. (Those who feel aroused simply call it by an acceptable name: righteous indignation, conviction, zeal perhaps, but never anger.)

"I'm not angry, only concerned," insisted Pastor Charles as he stood there in the sanctuary, rigid and stiff-jawed. Jake's neck glowed red against the black and white of his clerical collar. He smiled, but without parting his teeth. His eyes were flat, cold, distant. His knuckles shone white as he clenched the back of the pew in front of him. He stands there yet in my museum of memories—Jake Charles, a "correct" model of anger management in the ministerial profession: "I'm not angry, only concerned." I've said it myself, often. Have you?

The Myth of the Angerless Minister

So I'm really pleased with myself as I drive back to the church from Al's house. The way I figure, I had listened patiently to Al's blistering attack on me, and I had not lost my cool. Even the fact that he chairs the pastoral committee didn't get to me at all.

I pull into the church parking lot, stop the car, and reach to shut off the engine. Only then do I notice how my hand is shaking—so severely that I fumble pulling the key from the ignition. My stomach feels cramped into a painful ball of wire.

Suddenly I realize: I'm angry. In fact I'm raging inside.

But I've nowhere to go with it, no one to talk to and find release. To unload on my secretary would be unfair, especially if the disagreement with Al should ever explode publicly. As a pastor, I'm alone with my pain.

Carl Fitzgerald is in his third year of pastoral ministry. Mounting tensions here in his first congregation are about to erupt within the church board. Whether Al's words are trigger or trumpet of the impending battle, young Carl's first major crisis is waiting in the wings—or, to be more precise, in the narthex.

Pastor Fitzgerald has reason to feel anger, but no occasion to express it. As his anxiety level rises, his effectiveness decreases because his vital energies are being misdirected. They are being channeled into anger emotions, resentment feelings, and frustration responses. His emergency energies are all needed to control, contain, and conceal the hostility. He has little strength left to power his interactions with others. Carl has become a pastoral tragedy just waiting to happen. No release seems available. No renewal of attitudes and responses seems likely to ensue. He feels trapped by his people's expectations of pastoral virtue and ministerial perfection, caught by his own needs to conform to the congregation's demands in order to earn approval.

According to a venerable myth of congregational life, "the effective pastor knows how to absorb others' anger without contributing any of his or her own." As anger accumulates in the congregation's emotional system, it is the pastor who is called to defuse it, to neutralize the hostile acidity in the manner of an effervescent agape-seltzer. Pastors are supposed to be able to absorb more hostility than other professionals and to be without anger themselves.

The myth is worth satirizing. A pastor who has no access to the emotions of anger is a gentle caricature of full personhood. A minister stripped of all option for expressing legitimate anger is constricted into something less than true humanity.

When clergypersons are unaware of their inner hostility— or unwilling to dare experiencing such threatening feelings— they eliminate a rich part of their responsiveness to others. The result is not only a personal loss but also an impoverishment of the community they mean to serve.

The myth of the angerless pastor has its roots in a long and distinguished tradition. The traditional dualism of religious piety tended to split feelings, attitudes, and emotions into two categories, labeled "good" and "bad." Warm and gentle emotions—love, kindness, patience—were classified as good. The cold emotions, such as hate, or the hot emotions, like anger, were categorized as bad. Spiritual development was understood as a process of eradicating the bad emotions and cultivating the good. Eliminate the negative, accentuate the positive, press toward perfection—such was the program of traditional piety.

Interpreted on the basis of this dualistic frame of reference, the Pauline injunctions to put off the old nature with its destructive behaviors and to put on the new being with its constructive responses were easily misinterpreted.* An obvious identification of "the flesh and its desires" with inner hostility or anxiety-arousing emotions only confirmed the dualism and served to give anger and its associated negative feelings a consistently bad press.

The mind-body split carried this simplistic either-or perspective even further. According to traditional ascetic doctrine, mind must be renewed by spirit, and body must be repressed by will. The view persisted from Plato to Augustine to Descartes to Freud, even while evolving a rich and varied vocabulary: reason versus emotion, spirit versus flesh, mind versus body, civilization versus instincts.

The holistic view of emotions, on the other hand, has equal antiquity but hardly the theological popularity of the dualistic view. Careful theological, philosophical, and psychological thinkers have viewed humans holistically, seeking to integrate the positive and negative poles of emotional and rational response. In their view, openness to experiencing the self invites awareness of all emotive responses, whether hot or cold, distant or close. The freedom to be genuine and spontaneous in positive responses opens the possibility of equal awareness and expression also of the negative responses. By the same token, to restrict the anger side is to constrict the loving side. To eliminate either pole automatically limits the other.

Persons on guard against any possible admission of anger must carefully screen any and all emotional responses in tense situations. The spontaneous exuberance of uncontrolled love and affection gets filtered out along with the impulse to express irritation. What emerges is a certain stolidity, with a stiff and stultifying air of proper piety. Life loses the spark of immediate presence. When all responses have to be fully edited and approved by the conscientious censor within, human relationships become distant. They take on a kind of secondhand quality. The public person functions only as proxy for the unseen executive conscience, who is "unfortunately unavailable for immediate encounter."*

The central issue, then, is not *whether* one experiences negative emotions, but *how*; not *if* one dare become angry, but in what *way*. To be fully aware of one's anger or hate, and to be free to integrate it in ways that are both powerful and respectful, is to be vitally alive. To be truly alert to effective ways of channeling these emotions creatively is to be authentically present with others and prizing of the self. There are no good or bad feelings; feelings simply *are*. Moral choice begins not with the experiencing of feelings, but with their expression.

Unfortunately it is the dualistic rather than the holistic view that largely prevails today. It is still the unquestioned judgment of "common sense" among good religious people in our parishes. Clear and simple divisions of good feelings and bad feelings, of nice emotions and not-so-nice emotions, are used to make moral judgments on self and others. Thus the negative feelings are contained and the positive contaminated by these unrecognized reserves. Obviously, "good" pastors too have only "good" emotions.

The Quest for Perfection

The religious drive to eliminate negative responses and elaborate on positive emotions has frequently focused its demands on the religious leader. In Western societies the professional religious person is traditionally ordained to symbolize holiness, victory, perfection, beatitude, or whatever title is given a high-virtue/low-vice position. A church may expect its minister to embody the dream of sinlessness which the members cannot themselves attain but nonetheless righteously require of their representative.

Such demands are especially familiar to women pastors. For centuries women generally have felt the oppression of similar taboos. It is not "ladylike" (virtuous) or "feminine" (Christian) to show anger. After all, it is the woman's job (pastor's job) to keep peace in the family (community). A special vocabulary of whip-words is used to intimidate: "She's being bitchy, castrating, nagging, aggressive, masculine."

Thus for a woman pastor the taboos are doubled, perhaps even squared. At the same time, her reasons for anger—centuries of Christian tradition supporting abusive dominance, and millenia of male-defined theology—are even greater. Anger at injustice and indignation at inhumanity are a major part of a pastor's mission. Perhaps only women pastors can perceive the injustice accurately and confront it rightly. Confronting systemic injustice, and thereby releasing the pent-up pain, is a monumental task for which clergy are frequently ill prepared. Traditional counsel recommends only the use of strategies for containing or controlling the anger, rather than offering alternate ways of creatively channeling it.

These containment, concealment, or total control strategies are commonly called defense mechanisms. They serve as a protection against becoming aware of one's frustration and admitting one's confusion openly to another.* These defense mechanisms of ours operate in various ways with different people and in different situations: "I ought not to be angry. There's no place in the ministry for a person who can't control personal irritation. If I let anger show, I'm just no good." These are the sounds of guilt from a powerful conscience using the strategy of repression.

"Anger? What anger? I'm just *concerned* about Dave and the way he treats people. Actually I'm sorry for him. I feel nothing but compassion for him when he cuts into me with his vicious and vitriolic criticisms." The feelings revealed by the closing words show hostility hidden under a pious protest of positive emotions. This practice of calling bitter feelings sweet and renaming hate as love is a strategy of reaction formation.

"I'm not angry. Tom doesn't bother me at all. No way will I let him have the satisfaction of getting me rankled. Who does he think he is to imagine that his objections could upset me?" Irritation is being denied, internalized, and preserved. Intensified irritation is the probable outcome of this strategy of denial.

"I've nothing against Gloria, but she is obviously out to get me. Well, we'll see about that! It's going to be either me or her. This church isn't big enough for both of us. She's just like Vivian in my last pastorate, only this time she'll be the one to go, not me." Notice here that the minister's anger is being attributed to the parishioner in accusations of plotting, rejecting, and power politicking. But notice too who is actually doing the blaming, rejecting, and plotting for exclusion. Like movie operators using their own projector to show their own plot on some other person's screen, the minister is here projecting.

"I just refuse to think about the irritating person. I stay out of contact with irritating situations. I tune out the irritation and bury myself in other activities. I can handle almost anything this way." Dismissing the problem from consciousness and withdrawing from the problem situation may eliminate anger and anxiety from present awareness, but it only stores them up in the memory or recycles them into other responses. To pocket the problem until later is to employ the strategy of isolation.

"I can't stand people who talk about other people's problems. I can't tolerate gossip. By the way, will you promise to remember in your prayers one of our elders who is sleeping with his secretary? If word of this affair ever got out, the scandal would be awful." What good, moral people despise as unacceptable in others—in this case gossip—they may find ways, acceptable ways, of doing themselves through the strategy of displacement.

Repression, reaction formation, denial, projection, isolation, displacement—all are common defense mechanisms. They constitute a rich assortment of strategies promising the containment and total control of anger. But their promises are only promises! Negative containment strategies are at best purely temporary solutions. Positive channeling is the more effective means for utilizing anger creatively. Attempts to contain all negative responses tend only to recycle the frustration by converting it into more covert and corrosive forms of anger. So the pastor who presumes or is presumed to be without anger is in fact on the way not toward perfection but toward tragedy.

Nice Pastors Not So Nice

The sanctions against open recognition of anger and other negative emotions lead many pastors to internalize their frustrations and present a habitual nice-guy/nice-gal front to their parishioners. Most persons in crisis are grateful to have a nice, supportive person around on whose shoulder they can unload a portion of their stress. But constant support from an incessantly "nice" person also creates uneasiness and often eventual mistrust.*

Chronic niceness in a pastor tends to elicit comparable niceness in others, with the result that negative feelings are not readily shared and resentments accumulate. When the pastor's controls are finally overloaded, temper outbursts occur, with mixed results. While they may release momentary tension, they can create subsequent frustration and further strain the relationships.

Habitual niceness inhibits the free expression of natural responses. It prohibits easy discussion of differences, making it hard to initiate frank interchange. Participants are kept on guard by the fear that their relationship could not survive a spontaneous hassle if one should erupt.

Professional niceness maintains distance between persons. The other person is held at arm's length. Irritations are handled with a "soft touch," and the more intimate levels of trust and risk go unexplored. When anxiety rises, negotiation of disagreements leads to surface solutions, and real contact rarely happens.

Perpetual niceness creates patterns of denial in relationships, and the pastor's denying style can help set the tone for a whole community's "united front" method of suppressing conflict. Since group members are denied opportunity to talk their way through grievances or misunderstandings, depressive symptoms are frequently triggered or intensified in those predisposed toward devaluing themselves.

There is a niceness that is terminal. Terminal niceness can so atrophy a person's responsiveness to others that meaningful conversation ends, significant relationships become superficial, and ministry is largely a matter of maintenance and routine. Some of the "nicest" churches can be quite dead.

It's not nice to play nice, especially for pastors. Depriving others of a whole and fully aware person against whom to test themselves can limit their opportunities for growth in personhood. Failure to offer an effective model of channeling anger is failure to provide a creative alternative people can add to their behavioral repertoire. The two most frequently used anger styles, carried over from childhood, afford for most of us our two main ways of responding to frustration: hold it in or hand it out. But neither promotes human happiness, neither is productive in achieving satisfactory resolutions, and neither is helpful for creating community. It is hardly "nice" of pastors to sanction such responses by the anger style they personally and professionally model to the congregation.

Managing Anger

The angry pastor generally has several alternatives when it comes to identifying and expressing anger. Indeed, three key options for anger management seems to recur regularly:

(1) Internalize frustration. Learn the art of swallowing it, stomaching it, digesting it, "forgetting" it. Hold the anger inside and hope that you may be that rare exception to all the rules, the one who can minimize stress and its harmful side effects while maximizing the rewards of "peacemaking."

(2) Externalize frustration. Develop private means of ventilating tension. Punch a bag in the basement. Keep a rubber bat in the closet to pound pews in an empty church. Emblazen a full set of imprinted golf balls with the names of problem parishioners. Or master the more public styles of cloaking hostility in satire, humor, moralistic preaching, and politicking.

(3) Actualize frustration. Accept the risk of valuing your anger energies and channeling their power for impactful negotiation. Celebrate their vitality in intimate contact with others and utilize their potential for creative change. And with it all, accept the misunderstanding of those about you who continue to want less humanness and more niceness.

There may be other alternatives as well, but a continuing focus on these three may help you to sort out your own styles and preferences in anger management. Affirm the possibility of learning to think in new ways. Try to feel in new and different ways by canceling old demands and clearing up old resentments. Discover that present tensions need no longer be contaminated by past troubles, or new challenges misinterpreted as old conflicts. Recognize that clear thinking can help to clean up feelings.

Having realized the high personal cost of internalizing anger, and reckoned with the exorbitant professional costs of externalizing it, the minister can lead out in turning anger to creative ends. Mature persons seeking to experience their full selves, to express a balanced range of healthy emotions, and to actualize all they are created and called to be surely need models they can see, behaviors they can incorporate, and examples they can digest and assimilate in the creation of Christian personality. The pastor has a distinctive opportunity for ministry in this area.

Wholeness in the experiencing of one's own anger and effectiveness in the expressing and facilitating of others' anger can contribute toward a freeing of the community to deal creatively with its pain as real pain rather than converting it into painful interpersonal conflicts or intergroup combat. Again the pastor is in a unique position to facilitate resolution and growth if anger is regarded not as an exit signal for the minister but as an excitement to ministry.

Chapter Paradigm

The mythic pastor without anger
Will haunt the Christian community
As long as such a half-person is needed
To symbolize our dream of eliminating
Our shadow selves with their threatening violence.

The whole pastor with expressive warmth,
Warm love, warm anger, warm loving anger
Can model the integrity the community wants
And facilitate the growth of wholeness
In balanced selfhood, peoplehood, and new humanity.

The constructive pastor, the creative community
Can move beyond denial and distortion,
Dropping surface niceness and superficial distancing;
Each can meet the other with candor and caring,
Exciting each other to maturity and ministry.

2. The Aware Pastor—
Owning Energies

A motorcycle is sitting smack on the center line, waiting for the light to turn, as I pull alongside in my Datsun for a quick right on red. As I brake to my usual rolling stop, the cyclist leans over and raps harshly on my window. Suddenly I remember: cyclists hate drivers who sneak by them in tight spots.

Instantly my stomach knots with fear. The sound of an angry fist on the window beside my ear conjures up the fantasy of a leather-jacketed assailant shattering my window in rage. I suddenly feel equal rage in response.

I turn quickly and to my surprise see not the expected easy rider, but a fellow member of my own congregation. Alex's eyes widen as he recognizes me. Then we both break into laughter.

Three blocks down the street, I am still laughing exaggerately. "How do you like that?" I ask my wife rhetorically. "Mild old Alex was beating my window in!" Hilarious!

I'm high on adrenalin. Indeed, it was the instant flash of adrenalin that stimulated this kaleidoscope of emotions in the first place: intense fear followed by catastrophic fantasy, then anger, surprise, humor, elation, and now euphoria. The emotions fluctuate with each shift in my perception of the events.

Appraisal and Arousal

Appraisal is a function of the mind—how I *see* what is happening. Arousal is a function of the body—how I *feel* what is happening. The two go hand in hand. The mind appraisal interprets my body arousal and supplies identifying labels called feelings.

As my appraisal of the situation changes rapidly from "I'm being attacked" to "good old Alex got caught by the pastor," the emotion labels I apply to my experience alter at equal speed. The high level of body arousal that follows a burst of adrenal energy provides an overstimulated sequence of emotions to intensify my perceptions of what is happening.

Seeing the cyclist as hostile and negative, I name the aroused feeling "fear." The adrenal energies are constricting my chest, shortening my breathing, choking my throat.

Then I hear violence in his blows on the window. I see him as attacking, and I label the aroused feeling "anger." My face is flushed, my stomach knotted, and my hands clutch at the steering wheel.

Suddenly I recognize the cyclist as a member of my own church. I realize that the one confronting me is an old friend, and I feel relief. I breathe deeply, brush the moisture from my forehead, and begin to laugh.

Driving away, I see him as a parishioner who is probably embarrassed himself about coming on so strongly to the pastor, and I experience the arousal as feeling amused, in fact, elated. I'm chuckling at the incongruous situation. I'm euphoric.

Mind and body, appraisal and arousal, thinking and feeling are the two interdependent poles of the whole experience. Indeed, experiencing is a blend of both: the mind appraisal (symbolized awareness, perception, cognition, thinking) and the body arousal (presymbolized awareness, affective valuation, feeling). What we commonly call emotion actually represents a composite of both. A physiological state of arousal combines with a cognitive assessment of the situation to form an emotion.

Either may come first. Most often, the energies of body arousal are explained and directed by the mind's appraisal. Feelings are labeled according to the opinion held at the moment. In the next moment, however, new data may alter opinions, and feeling labels will change as arousal and appraisal blend in ever new and differing combinations.*

Perception and Emotion

My dentist, giving me a shot of Novocain in preparation for minor dental work, by mistake inserts the needle into a vein. As the full injection enters my bloodstream, my pulse instantly doubles, my respiration accelerates, my face reddens, and my abdomen feels warm, then tight and fluttering.

"What was in that shot?" I demand, feeling the sudden physiological arousal.

"Novocain."

"And?"

"And a little adrenalin to tighten the tissue and prevent bleeding."

"So you gave me a shot of adrenalin straight into the vein?" My mind is working at double speed. Detectivelike, I'm deciphering my body signals and the dentist's noncommittal responses. "Does anyone ever die of cardiac arrest from adrenalin shock?"

"It happens."

Instant anger blinds me. The clown! He gave me the needle without checking to see where he was putting it. I could throttle him! Perception: the incompetent bungler could have killed me. Emotion: rage.

But the symptoms soon stabilize. Hey, the old ticker's working fine. So I'm a little overstimulated—so what? Perception: I'm alive and well and high on adrenalin. Emotion: relief.

I begin to reflect. What if the cardiac shock had been too massive? Imagine the blow to Nancy and the girls out there in the waiting room. Perception: loss of self, life, family relationship. Emotion: sadness and grief.

But humor too breaks through. Imagine the dentist reporting to my family: "I saved the tooth, but lost the patient." Perceiving the ridiculous, the emotion is hilarity.

The body arousal caused by this chemical accident is identical with that caused by the automatic burst of adrenalin triggered by some threat or frustration. Knowing the source of the intense physiological arousal, however, permits me to take control of the excitement and direct the emotional energies in useful ways.

As I choose how I will see the dentist and his error, I am choosing, indirectly, how I will feel about it. I cannot directly choose my emotions as such. I cannot say, "I will feel happy —so, I am happy. Now I will feel sad—ergo, I am sad. I will feel angry—beware, I am angry! I will feel happy again— *voilà,* I am happy." I can choose my perceptions, however, and each selected perception may then evoke its consequent emotion.*

While perception evokes emotion, the reverse is equally true: emotion may direct perception. Suppose that on the morning after my episode with Alex I'm sitting behind the wheel of my Datsun when a motorcycle pulls up beside me, just behind the driver's field of peripheral vision. Although I am deeply involved in a discussion with my wife and quite oblivious to the cyclist's presence, the sound of the motorcycle engine and exhaust is not lost on me altogether. I am not consciously aware of its proximity, but my preconscious mind appraisal is already stimulating a repeat of yesterday's body arousal. I snap at Nancy more angrily than our argument might have called for, and as the light changes and the cyclist roars by me on the left, my body flinch clues me to the intensity of my feelings. They seem to be out of all proportion to the gravity of our present debate and are perhaps as much dependent on yesterday as today.

Mind appraisal and body arousal can each trigger the other. Both are involved in most experience. It is mind appraisal, however, that actually labels the experience. In any situation of threat or frustration, we react emotionally only to the extent that we also experience a state of excitation. When the body arousal is initiated by a shot of adrenalin, the mind appraisal will label the experience either as a physiological response or as an emotion. It is a simple physiological response if the datum on the shot is known, for example, externally administered by mistake. It is an emotion—anger, euphoria, sadness, fear—if the datum on the shot is not known, that is, if it is internally triggered by the relational dynamics operative at the time of the arousal.*

Mind appraisal may be either conscious or preconscious. That is, we do our labeling in consequence either of our symbolized perceptions or our unsymbolized perceptions, often called subceptions. If I am to appraise situations accurately, I need to be aware of both.

Multilevel Perceptions

> The moment the budget committee came to the item called pastor's salary, I saw the vice-chairperson push his chair back a few inches and tune out of the discussion altogether. Greg is also head of the pastoral committee. I had carefully planned ahead just how I would go about making my request for an appropriate raise, but now my mind suddenly went blank. It was nothing that was said. I just felt wiped out by Greg's gesture. There was an awkward pause, during which I could feel the anger starting to grow in my gut. Someone moved that the pastor receive the standard inflationary increase. The motion passed. I excused myself, went to the john, and vomited.

What happened inside Harley Fisher to stifle all normal expression of thoughts and feelings? The signals Pastor Fisher had perceived were in themselves hardly cause for such intense alarm.

Greg Peters had withdrawn emotionally, and without their vice chairperson's vital input the budget committee had stumbled along, ill at ease in deciding on the pastor's annual income. When someone proposed a solution, they were all relieved and immediately adopted it. No perceived cause for alarm, right? True—unless the small signals had a significance not readily apparent except to Pastor Fisher.

Signals subceived are not as simple as signals perceived. They do not readily meet the eye. On three earlier occasions in finance committee meetings the pastor had seen Greg withdraw into a foreboding funk, sit silently on a long fuse, and then without warning explode into cold fury. In the melee that followed, the surgical edge of Greg's words had sliced through relationships cleanly but without respect for anything or anyone else. When it was all over, who recalled the signals that had preceded the altercations? Nobody. Not the pastor, not the committee members, not Greg himself, at least not consciously. Yet all of them now walked as if on eggs, and group anxiety visibly rose the moment Greg shifted the position of his chair.

"The incredible thing," remarked the pastor in later reflection, "is how similar Greg's threat of impending explosion is to my dad's way of tyrannizing Mom and us kids. Dad was like a brooding time bomb waiting for someone to trigger his rage. As a kid, I was often sick to my stomach for hours at a time, just from fear I guess."

Pastor Fisher's responses in the situation were directed not by his conscious perceptions of what was actually transpiring, but by his subceptions of the deeper meaning of it all. Data coming in from Greg's body language and from the behavior of the committee as a whole was interpreted in terms of the pastor's preconscious memories of his previous life under an authoritarian personality, his father. The resultant response was intimidation, withdrawal, anger, and conversion to bodily sickness, as in earlier childhood.

Mind appraisal occurs at many levels. There are conscious perceptions and there are preconscious subceptions. A subceived appraisal, as in the case of Pastor Fisher, may actually be unavailable to the person even though it becomes a powerful source of anger arousal.

Where there is a rich legacy of unresolved relationships from the past buried deep inside a person, puzzling internal conflicts often surface in situations which repeat the threatening signals of old. Body arousal may well up in response to even one slight signal. Greg's silent, stiff withdrawal automatically triggered the pastor's anger, which was rising to meet the expected anger in the parishioner. When neither party understands what is happening, neither is likely to make a useful response. Since the real issue being negotiated is like an iceberg, only partially available to awareness, the main concerns arise not as thoughts but as feelings, and arouse the body with intense emotion.

The Importance of Awareness

Awareness is the key. That which is beyond my awareness is not available to me for conscious choice or deliberate decision making. It is nonetheless present and powerful in the interpersonal process, appearing as feelings, urges, impulses, intuitions, or understandings. When these conflict or are grandiose in their expectations, they stimulate intense arousal.

Bringing to awareness that of which I am unaware can be a long process, but it need not be a confusing one. As each important bit of unawareness surfaces, appreciate it, face it, own it, deal with it. Always be alert for the next significant item that may rise from the deep storehouse of memory reserves. Be particularly alert to disturbing feelings, for they suggest the active presence of such items, things from beyond the pale of awareness that can condition our perceptions and trigger our arousals. These we must learn to discern, appreciate, own, and seek to understand.* As we deepen awareness and own as much of our experience as possible, angry persons can be freed to be responsible toward themselves and others. That was Pastor Fisher's experience:

> If I had let myself see what Greg was actually doing by freezing, withdrawing, and threatening the whole group, if I had been aware of it instead of denying and ignoring it— as I had learned to do with my father—then I could have identified my own anger alarm. I might have relaxed and even eased the whole situation with a few affirmative and confrontive words. If such comments were to trigger an outburst, I think the group could deal with it; they could handle open anger. But the silent threat of an impending annihilation that no one dares to name openly and face candidly can be devastating.
>
> My body seemed to read accurately what was happening, but my mind refused to appraise the meaning of the body's arousal. I couldn't see what was transpiring because I chose not to trust my own organism and its inner wisdom. All I

wanted was to control the rage boiling up within. That's
what Greg was doing too, overcontrolling. We got nowhere!

When my immediate response to anger is an all-out effort
to contain and control such negative emotions, the inner dynamics follow a common pattern: I deny what is being sensed,
repress what is being felt, and convert the inner stress into
body dysfunctions.* If, on the other hand, my focus is on
appreciating and channeling anger as it occurs, the awareness of body arousal may be deepened and the accuracy of
mind appraisal improved. Owning my anger can bring body
foresight and mind insight together in such a way that each
can inform the other. Then the organism's response and the
mind's ability can be integrated into a wholeness called responsibility, the ability to respond congruently.

Anger and Wholeness

As the pattern of denial can cut persons off from themselves, reducing awareness and limiting integration, so can
movement in the opposite direction lead to enhanced awareness and growth toward wholeness. Anger can be positively
productive, and the factors in that process are worth enum-
erating:

(1) Appreciating. I prize my freedom to be fully me. I
value my ability to respond with my whole self. I am equally
worthful whether raging or calm within, whether perceiving
positively or negatively, whether hostile toward others or hap-
pily in harmony with them. I appreciate my anger.

(2) Trusting. I trust my own responsibility, my capacity
to respond. I allow my responses to flow freely. I feel, speak,
and act spontaneously. Rejection can occur as well as acceptance. I go with the flow of thought and feeling until I
find it ineffective or unsatisfying. I trust my anger.

(3) Owning. I own my own thoughts, feelings, words, and
actions. They are my chosen responses to my own perceptions
of a situation. It is not your action but mine that determines
my reaction. *You* do not make me angry; *I* make me angry
at you. I own my anger.

(4) Experiencing. I am not able to choose emotions di-

rectly: as I (*a*) perceive you rejecting, attacking, or frustrating me, I (*b*) demand that you respond instead with the behaviors I prescribe, and I (*c*) feel anger. So my choice may be indirect, based on a perception, but that is how the process occurs, and I accept it, I own it. I experience my anger.

(5) Awareness. I discover that I often have negative feelings even before becoming aware of such perceptions and demands. Body arousal often signals their presence. I am learning to listen more carefully, discern more wisely, focus more consciously. I am aware of my anger.

(6) Growing. I celebrate my responsibility to own my anger and arousal, evoked by my own appraisal, the result of my own choice. Affirming my own perceptions, owning my own experience, I can choose to cancel or modify my demands, or appropriately to articulate my desire for changes that could make our relationship more mutually satisfying. Anger management helps me to grow in responsibility, the ability to respond in mature and effective ways.

These are the factors that tie anger to wholeness. The sequence of course is not invariable, but together they integrate arousal and appraisal, mind and body, perception and subception. The process of achieving this wholeness in life is a "win some/lose some" series of experiences. Sometimes I exercise myself with gratifying balance and sometimes I find myself only partially successful in appreciating, trusting, owning, and enjoying self-awareness.*

The Question of Ownership

When the right to be angry and the responsibility for being angry are reclaimed, anger can be productive. When the responsibility for anger is attributed to others, anger is still explosive, but fruitless. Much depends on the source of my anger.

Anger Directed By Others

Other-directed anger denies ownership of the anger and attributes it elsewhere. It operates from basic beliefs about outside control:

You make me angry.

So your action is responsible
For my feelings of pain.

So you are responsible
To make me feel right again.

So you must change
In the way I prescribe.

So I will resent you,
Reject you,
Force you to meet my demands
Until you shape up
And make things right again.

Such other-directed anger is essentially powerless. It has lost the power of its own agency. Totally dependent on the other's response, it awaits the other's choice to resolve the tension. If I give you the power to make me angry, to call out or control my emotions, then I am crediting you—or blaming you—for my inner being and my inner responses. I am giving you the power over my future responses as well. I am simply left waiting, feeling my demands, threatening you with my hostility, but quite unable to alter the situation or the responses. And as I am impotent to be me, I am also powerless to invite you to be truly you.

Blaming-anger of this kind is barren and impotent. As anger it is still a potent emotion, but because it is diffused ineffectively in fingering imagined causes out there in the environment, the real demands within the anger go unexpressed and unnegotiated. Crediting the anger response to the environmental stimulus that was allowed to trigger it, the you-make-me-angry pastor is stuck. There is no place to go— unless the blaming pays off with the other person accepting the guilt and trying to "make the mad one glad again."

Anger Directed By Self

Self-directed anger operates from an ownership position that takes responsibility for the emotional content and clearly reports the demands for change in the relationship. It too proceeds from certain basic assumptions:

> I make me angry.
>
> So your emotion or action
> Does not control my reaction.
>
> So I am responsible
> For my feelings and actions.
>
> So I cancel my demand
> That you change as I prescribe.
>
> So I will report
> How I see you,
> What I feel toward you,
> Where I am in our differences,
> What I am willing to do
> In getting together again.

Owning my perceptions, clarifying my demands, and taking appropriate action frees me to reclaim the power to feel, think, choose, and to assert myself as a person. I can freely affirm my anger feelings, assert—or cancel—my anger demands, and respond to others in aware choice making.

But, you may say, if I own full responsibility for my anger, what about those situations in which another intentionally irritates me, willfully attacks my known weak spots, or deliberately violates me as a person? In such moments I can assert that "not you, but I am making me angry," but is not such an assertion only a matter of semantics? What power is present in such affirmation?

No, it is not merely a matter of semantics. Yes, there is

power in the affirmation of ownership. Even in circular relationships, I can move freely only as I lay claim to my own anger and see my response as open to choice. If you test me and I take the anger bait, then it is still not you who are making me angry. For seeking to bait me, you are responsible. But it is I who choose, consciously or unconsciously, to take the anger bait; for that I am responsible. And if I continue to take the bait as often as you offer it, I am either refusing to learn from my experience or I am getting some rewards from my bait snatching. However, the cycle can be interrupted! If I can see the game we are playing, if I can reorganize the cycle of baiting, blaming, and rebaiting, then I can perhaps also choose new ways of responding to you. The important thing is to clear up the ownership question and know who is responsible for the anger.

Driving absentmindedly, I am oblivious to the road sign and miss the turn as Route 66 swings right. Instantly my wife says, "I'd have turned right back there." Anger surges up in me. "Sure, sure," I want to say, "I'd have turned right back there too if I'd known then what we both know now."

"She baits me," I tell myself, "she hooks my anger and I'm too slow to interrupt it."

Later, as I rerun the scene with her in slow motion, I see who is baiting whom. As we enter the intersection, *she* is not watching the road; supposedly, *I* am. As I belatedly see the road sign, my shoulders jerk, I grimace and flinch. She, alerted by my body language, looks for the occasion and, seeing the sign, says in recognition, "I'd have turned right back there." And now I'm angry. Who is baiting whom? We are both in cyclical anger. As the awareness dawns, we break up in laughter.

And the next time I miss a turn, I chuckle, "I've just done it again!" We both laugh. We have reason to laugh: we're unhooked at one more point. Owning our own anger, claiming its direction for ourselves rather than blaming it on others, we can respond; we don't have to react. And there is a difference.

Reacting or Responding

"How was your week?" asked Ed. Ed McGowen is chairperson of the pastoral committee, and before I know it his innocent after-service question triggers a flood of statistics on my part. Instantly I'm reporting on the number of house calls made, meetings attended, hospital visits completed, and pastoral interviews conducted. It's like I'm on trial. I don't know why, but when he asks me about my work, I'm instantly guilty. Then, later, I rage inside. I'm reacting.

As a reactor, a person automatically replies in kind to another's behavior. The dominant language is either accusing or excusing: "You make me . . ." or "You won't let me . . ." The emotions experienced are automatic reactions to another's pain or joy. There is little freedom to choose. I react as I have to.

Freedom from being maneuvered into such cyclical binds comes with the ability to respond responsibly. I become a responder by claiming my own emotions and directing them. As a responder I can affirm in clear language: "I am . . . I feel . . . I want . . ." I can be spontaneous and responsible without being manipulated from without. I can be angry when I choose and, when I choose, I can interrupt my anger reactions and create new ways of responding to another.*

Again it is largely a question of ownership. We react when we believe that our behavior is determined by others. We respond when we affirm that our own choice and change can interrupt the old cycles of learned and automatic conflict. Repentance is a matter of owning up to the old ways of the past and choosing new ways for the future. Awareness and ownership make repentance possible. Reaction denotes bondage. Freedom comes with the ability to respond.

Chapter Paradigm

Body arousal excites————Emotion
Mind appraisal interprets——Perception
Awareness unites ————Integration
Responsibility directs ———Liberation

3. The Insightful Pastor— Channeling Anger

"In the white trunks, weighing in at 225 pounds, the Reverend Mr. Ned Porter. In the black trunks, weighing 175, Stan Lusty, minister of music. This championship fight is scheduled to go a full ten rounds."

That's how the pastoral committee should have announced it when I came to Park Avenue last year. Stan Lusty and I have been circling each other in the ring ever since, sparring, feinting, and jabbing. But we never touch leather: I, unwilling to admit that I am furious with his theatrics; he, never saying an angry word. The resentment between us is now so vicious there's no safe place to start.

Pastor Porter's analogy is an honest one. After eight months of move and countermove, bluff and rebuff, each man has invested high amounts of anger energy in the competition for top billing. Always smiling before the people, each sweetly upstages the other in what passes at Park Avenue Church for public worship. To avoid outbursts of anger the preacher and the music master evade each other, and the evasion produces only greater distance and distrust between them. The pastor's imaging of the relationship in terms of the fight ring suggests a beginning of insight into what is really at stake.

Recognition of Anger

Crucial for effective working relationships on any team is an atmosphere of openness to the sharing of negative as well as positive feelings and feedback. Such openness is indispensable for joint ministry. When the church staff is teaching values, facilitating growth, and celebrating wholeness in other persons, these same staff members must also be experiencing these same things for themselves, and in their relationships with their associates as well, or the contradiction soon becomes apparent and intolerable. What is needed in the first instance for Pastor Porter and Mr. Lusty is an honest recognition of the anger that exists in each and an openness to the free and candid expression of that anger.

Openness involves a willingness to risk and is directly related to the level of trust existing between persons. Trust and risk go hand in hand. To risk open anger without building and testing out trust is to invite rejection or retaliation. Trust, however, can be tested only by actually venturing some anxiety-arousing feelings and perceptions. Trust is seldom experienced as genuine where anger is regarded as a threat or where the expression of anger is prohibited lest it lead to a rupture of relationship.*

Trust is increased when persons are allowed to feel and express negative as well as positive emotions. Such allowance bespeaks respect for the other as a whole human being. Genuine respect for the other's freedom to feel angry, think angry, and choose angry responses is bound to enhance trust. Such respect for the whole person insures that person the freedom to be spontaneous, open to valuing and owning all of the self.

Pastoral caring means a willingness to stand with others in their confused and angry thoughts, and to value their right to be angry even while not necessarily agreeing with all their angry demands. Pastoral caring implies a care of the whole person, not just of what is agreeable to or affirming for the pastor. Ministers who are willing to own their own personal anger and to respect anger in another, even when certain acts or behaviors of the other are deemed unacceptable, actually model openness and invite reciprocal candor on the part of the people they seek to serve.

Anger-shy pastors anxiously limit trust solely to the expression of positive emotions. A pastor's refusal to deal with another person's obvious anger can effectively inhibit that person's actions, words, and awareness of feelings. When I express my anger to you and find it totally ignored, or when I receive in return only positive responses that are quite unrelated to what is really happening between us, that stifles my ability to reflect and respond in depth. When feelings get tense and I cry out for involved response, your neutrality is not helpful. If you seek distance or act superior or self-sufficient when I am hurting, you actually function to deny the reality of my anger.* Thus the first thing to be understood in pastoral care as it relates to anger is the importance of openly recognizing anger where it exists. Ned Porter, pugilist, is struggling for that kind of openness.

Validation of Anger

"I'm fed up with my teachers bypassing me and running to the pastor to complain about the church school. You can have my resignation right now." Peter Duncan's eyes are on fire, his teeth clenched. His fury is that of a Christian education director whose direction has been undercut.

The pastor's neck grows red as she listens to Peter's explosion. Sparks glow in her own eyes. Sally Lane is so incensed by his personal attitude that she hardly attends to his articulated demands. "We do have a problem to discuss, Peter, but the problem is not your staff of teachers, it's your own attitude. You come storming in here full of anger at me and expressing your resentment. Until you can get rid of this hostility maybe resigning is a good idea."

Peter and Sally have a conflict all right, but what precisely is the root of that conflict? What is the most significant dynamic at work in their exchange? What is the point of most acute tension? The way Pastor Lane is getting triangled by dissatisfied teachers? Her willingness to have the teachers ventilate their anger about someone who is not present to hear their complaint? Her unwillingness to deal with the anger being expressed between the people who are present? Is it perhaps the pastor's denial of her own anger, and her rejection of the Christian education director's right to be angry?

Peter and Sally indeed have an immediate conflict over

their right to be angry with each other in the here and now, but that conflict is really of one piece with all the rest. If a person is unwilling to work through the anger that exists now (primary anger), then that energy is likely to be discharged in ventilation to a third party later (secondary anger). Such ventilation can perhaps release tension but it does not effect reconciliation. What Pastor Lane needs in the present instance is the insight to acknowledge the validity of Peter's strong feelings and his aroused expression of them.

Recognizing the validity of another's emotions requires an openness toward balanced, holistic emotions in the self and the other. Holistic emoting means that the person is free to feel negative as well as positive emotions. Feelings as such are acceptable, whether they are positive or negative, hot or cold, uniting or separating, accepting or rejecting, releasing or demanding. The significant issue is not which of the two poles the person may be experiencing and expressing at the moment, but in what way, to what end, and for what purpose? Is the emotion and its expression directed constructively toward the enhancement of human relationships, or destructively toward blocking them?

Holistic emoting is valid in human beings. It is a part of being human. In responding to another's anger, it is crucial that a pastor get free from the tendency automatically to prejudge another's angry feelings as invalid. Try these values on for size and fit:

(1) Emotions are neither good nor bad; they simply *are*. Moral judgment begins not with the feelings themselves, but with the behaviors and actions that ensue. The expression of confused or conflicting emotions is a valid privilege of personhood.

(2) Negative emotions are frequently the crucial pole of a person's experience. If they have been rejected, repressed, and recycled into other emotions, they deserve particularly sensitive respect and careful validation.

(3) The expression of negative emotions, having been sharply restricted in many situations and painfully distorted

in others, will be frequently mixed with attacking, blaming, judging, and rejecting statements. These must be coaxed or teased out. The anger itself can then be affirmed, clarified, focused, and resolved without allowing dysfunctional expressions to steal the show.

(4) The right to be angry responsibly is essential to people's experience of their own worth and human dignity. To violate this right is to invalidate the wholeness of that person. Persons are of irreducible value. They are worthful simply because they *are,* and no behavior can increase or decrease a person's value. I am irreducibly worthful, you are irreducibly worthful—whether we are angry or calm, succeeding or failing, hating or loving, apathetic or excited. We must prize each other's worth. We must free each other to experience and express that worth. We must create covenanting communities that value our mutual worth as whole persons. Unless we value the anger, we devalue the person. This is why the caring pastor nurtures the insight that anger is to be validated.

Clarification of Anger Demands

Recognition of the anger and validation of the person's right to be angry are properly followed by clarification of the anger demands. This is important because inside every feeling of anger there are demands that need to be spelled out. With this fact in mind, we can try a modified rerun of the Christian education director's confrontation with Pastor Sally Lane:

"I'm fed up with the teachers gossiping about me to you," begins Peter Duncan. "If you don't support me by bringing these people straight to me, you can have my resignation." His voice is sharp with anger.

"If I felt bypassed, I'd be angry too," the pastor replies instantly. "I've encouraged them to talk with you, Peter, but apparently my listening to them has had the opposite effect. Let's work at this until it's straightened out."

Clarification of angry feelings often requires combing out

the multiple strands among the demands and deciding what action is appropriate. These demands may involve needs that can be justly expressed and rightly pressed for resolution:

"Hear me; I have heard you."

"Respect me as I am respecting you."

"Stop taking me for granted; I am free to say either yes or no."

"Stop trying to control me; I prize my freedom to choose and to direct my own behavior."

Demands that are perceived as just can be asserted with clarity in the confidence that their appropriateness will be worthy of respect.

Some demands, however, may be unjust, irrational, and inappropriate to effective relationship:

"Obey me without question because I'm right."

"Do what I want when I want it simply because I want it."

"Do what I expect of you without my asking; know what I want by reading my mind."

Demands such as these may be quite unrealistic and unjust. As they are recognized, they can be canceled and more realistic demands chosen and negotiated.

Demands can get frightfully mixed up, the just with the unjust. The various strands can get hopelessly snarled when anger is hot and confused. To sort out anger demands and make choices about their importance and relative justice can be a painfully complex process, whether the anger be your own or that of another.

Anger is so obsessive in character that it tends to flood the awareness with an overwhelming concern about resolving the frustrating situation—with the result that too little time is invested in clarifying demands and too much time is spent in searching for solutions. It is a common mistake to invest one's major effort in working out a resolution before having clearly defined the problem. On the other hand, once the problem is seen clearly the solution will often emerge almost spontaneously.

Reflections in the journal of Pastor Ned Porter disclose his

own growth struggle as he seeks to clarify the anger demands
in his conflict with the minister of music:

> I find that when I think about Stan Lusty, my whole mind is
> inflamed and my body burns with it. I want that man out of
> the church. Or lacking that, I want out of this pastorate.
>   What is this rage I'm carrying inside like a demonic
> pregnancy? I can list all the ways he has upstaged everyone
> else with his dramatic razzle-dazzle. Sunday after Sunday,
> in what was supposed to be a service of worship . . .
>   I've got to get inside my own rage: what is it I'm demand-
> ing? I want to wish him out of existence, no, out of *my*
> existence.
>   But this anger is annihilating. To turn it creative, I want
> a chance to get things open with him. . . . I want him to
> finally see how the whole thing looks from my point of
> view. . . . I want to convert him to my point of view, of
> course . . . and I want a lot more—a public apology?
> Maybe, maybe not. A clear commitment for a working rela-
> tionship for the next six months? Yes, by all means.
>   Looking back over today's journal entry, I'm surprised by
> all the demands I have *not* made in my direct contacts with
> Stan, but *could* make if I were willing to do something with
> my anger.

Sorting out useful anger demands is Ned Porter's first step
toward a rapprochement with his fellow staff member. The
pastor needs to face and itemize his various wants, then focus
them in just and negotiable demands. "Don't exist" is hardly
negotiable; "Get out of my existence," almost as unreason-
able. Simple behavioral demands like "I want a chance at
open confrontation" or "I want my point of view expressed
and heard" may be perceived as both reasonable and just.
They may even be achievable, and, achieved, they can be
mutually beneficial. If the pastor can clarify his own anger
demands, he may also be able to respect the integrity of
Stan's—and even help Stan to sort them out and articulate
them clearly.

Simplification of Anger Demands

Helping others to express their anger demands is a process
that requires skill in simplifying the complex, focusing the
diffused, and sharpening what is blurred and confusingly

indistinct. A person who is not emotionally aroused can view the anger demands with sufficient distance to permit careful definition and cautious simplification. The person actually experiencing and expressing the anger, however, is more likely to resort to emotionally charged words that can be self-defeating.

How the anger demands are stated may determine what becomes of them, whether they succeed or fail. Demands articulated in generalized, broad, inclusive language tend to ask much and offer little. In the heat of anger it is often difficult, but nonetheless essential, not only to sort out the conflicting demands but also to focus them with simple clarity.

> I'll be seeing the principal in one hour, and I plan to give him a piece of my mind. I'm going to tell him how insensitive and unfair the school is in asking me to move into another teaching field with only two days to consider the offer before contract renewal. They're playing dirty with me, and they're going to hear it.

Steve Carney is a high school teacher being asked to give up his present chemistry classes and to teach biology courses for which he has no graduate preparation. Steve has just dropped by Pastor Nielsen's study during a lunch break, hoping to find release and support. He is obviously furious. His arguments are disconnected. He rambles on from central concern to peripheral gripe without the slightest awareness of how confused his thinking and expression are at the moment.

"Before you confront the principal," the pastor suggests, "use me for a rehearsal. Narrow the issues. Focus on what you really want." Steve does a trial run, then an improved rerun. "Now state your demand as neutrally as possible," the pastor suggests, "and then define its mutual benefits, its payoffs to both you and the school."

Thirty minutes later Steve Carney leaves Pastor Nielsen's study with his demands narrowed, his language neutral, and his arguments focused on a mutually beneficial outcome. The teacher has channeled his anger. He is ready to confront and to negotiate without breaking out into generalized hostility.

To channel anger is to simplify or focus the anger demands. Four elements are involved: (1) state the issue as a difference that arises among humans naturally; (2) do so in language that can be heard neutrally; (3) define the problem narrowly; and (4) let the goal be a solution that is agreed on mutually.

Describing Differences Naturally

I am not a "sickie" for reporting my anger demands. You are not a nut for specifying yours. Anger is a natural, normal response to the frustrations of living together.

That understanding is reinforced when we use natural categories for stating our anger demands instead of using disease language, medical or pathological labels. Anger is not a matter of insanity. Anger tensions are natural human processes, not illnesses. Differences and disputes between persons are a natural part of humanness, not a disorder. Conflict and competition are normal human passions, not a disability.

Angry conflict is the result of one person's thrust intersecting with that of another person. It is the task of the reconciling community—its natural task—to find ways of utilizing both thrusts for the maximum benefit of both persons and with a minimum of pain.

Respecting the naturalness of anger reduces the guilt cycle of "I'm angry, and I feel guilty that I'm angry, and I'm both angry and guilty that you see my anger." To interrupt this cycle, appreciate your own worth as an angry person, affirm the right of the other to be angry, and define the conflict, the divergences, the antagonistic feelings as naturally as possible. To channel anger is to describe the differences naturally.

Describing Differences Neutrally

Neutralize your language in defining the demands before you debate them. Select terms that can reduce rather than heighten tension.

It is possible, for example, to favor adverbs that describe how much (quantity) over adjectives that define what kind of (quality). A qualitative judgment like "I'm tired of your dominating our conversation and controlling our relationship!" can escalate tension. More neutral expressions are probably more helpful: "I think I've been too passive in our relationship." "My silence invites you to carry on more than your half of our conversation." "I'll be claiming equal time."

Any use of derogatory words exaggerates tensions. A label, for the recipient, can feel like libel. "I demand that you do something about your racism, your neurosis, your meanness" —such labels only escalate anxiety, evoke further anger, and accelerate defensive rage.

The neutral expression of anger can reduce the negative cycle of each reaction triggering another. When I am angry I sometimes fantasize gross injustices being done against me, I explode in similarly exaggerated countercharges, and I evoke equally defensive ventilation in return. To deescalate this spiral, I try to tone down the language inside my head and respond more neutrally to the other person's emotionally loaded phrases.

Pastors would do well to cultivate the practice—almost like a hobby—of collecting neutral expressions. Select a few low-threat formulas for offering angry feelings to others in a clear and simple way with a minimum of value judgment. Try lines like these: "The behavior you do which leaves me puzzled and irritated is . . ." "The viewpoint you just expressed has me confused and angry." "I'm getting so frustrated I'm not listening anymore; try me again." Hang onto the ones that seem authentic and work well for you. Practice them often.

When confronted angrily or judgmentally by another, formulate that person's demands in neutral words that may give little or no offense. Consider Pastor McGuire's way of turning a church-door explosion into productive sermon feedback and a counseling entree:

Jim: Pastor, that has to be one of the lousier sermons you've laid on us.

Pastor: Hi, Jim! . . . Sounds like you could use equal time to offer a different point of view.

Jim: I sure could. I think mixing the races is a kind of
         of mongrelization that has got to be stopped.
Pastor: We really do have contrasting points of view. When
         can we get together to check them out? I'm free
         over lunch tomorrow.

Pastors can develop skill in immediate redefining of demands in a neutral way, not in order to avoid angry emotions
but in order to focus clearly the demands within the explosion. Neutral language can sharply reduce the high anxiety
which threatens a blowup. Sometimes it will so reduce the
overload of anxiety that rational plans can be made for negotiation or debate of the issues.

Anger deserves such neutral expression and negotiation. To
treat an angry altercation as if it were intrinsically evil is to
block its natural progression, fog its normal meanings, and
sabotage its own rightful conclusion. To channel anger is to
define the anger demands neutrally.

Defining Differences Narrowly

Think small. Focus the problem as narrowly as possible. To
see the anger issue as the outcropping of a large, underlying
stratum of impossible differences, as representing two contrasting and intractable world views, is to enlarge the field of battle
to unmanageable proportions. Anger may indeed well up from
unsurveyed depths that defy description, but its management
and resolution in any instance call for precision and limitation
of focus.

I once heard a pastor tell of an unforgettable encounter with
an angry youth. The student seemed to be challenging the
status quo in all of its aspects. The pastor's description was
equally memorable: "This, in miniature, is a demonstration of
the deterioration of all youth-adult relationships, the widening
generation gap, the emergence of a hostile counterculture, the
collapse of traditional Christian moral values, the triumph of
a relativistic ethic, and the decline of Western civilization."

Pastor Benner was only offering a neat and in some ways
reasonable analysis of "the sociocultural impact on moral-

theological trends of generational change." The effect, however, was to augment the conflict to unmanageable proportions. The ability to generalize, to see the universal implications of human situations, is a useful skill in dispassionate analysis of certain situations, but not in anger resolution.

Narrow definition of the anger demands can often reverse the otherwise expanding shock waves of rage: "I am angry about your putting me down, I see our whole relationship as distasteful and rejecting, I reject you, I break off communications, I feel the whole world is against me." To reverse this ever-expanding cycle or exchange it for an ever-contracting one can swing the focus of anger demands from the general to the specific, from the impossible to the possible.

In dealing with anger, my own or that of another person, it is important to focus the anger demands and limit the conflict to its central components. The core problem needs to be discerned, the chief complaint isolated. Channeling anger requires that we define differences and demands narrowly.

Defining Differences Mutually

Angry demands are interpersonal matters. Where a relationship encounters difficulty, it is improbable that the disturbing element can be accurately defined in terms of its being one person's problem. Indeed, it is unlikely that any conflict will involve demands from only one side of the hassle. It takes two to tangle.

Similarly, conciliation takes two or more to make it complete. To see the difficulty as a joint problem is already a long step on the way which leads to change and mutual satisfaction. If the problem is to be truly solved, both persons need to be satisfied. Stating demands in an "I win/you lose" style is seldom useful in building relationships. The fact is that both can win when one or both persons work for a resolution in which mutual respect grows and increased trust emerges naturally from the negotiation. Both persons are freed to end the reciprocal blaming, both are invited fully to state their needs and demands.

Admitting that the anger situation happened between two

of us, and that two of us are taking responsibility for a joint solution, leads to the best resolution.* From the standpoint of both the problem and the solution, mutuality needs to be acknowledged. Channeling requires that we define the differences mutually.

Negotiation

When anger demands are accepted naturally, described neutrally, defined narrowly, and understood mutually, they have been channeled to the point where negotiation is possible. Fruitful negotiation is the purpose and goal of all the channeling.

Stan Lusty, the minister of music at Park Avenue Church, finally came to realize that eight months of distance, avoidance, and covert messages from the new minister had taken away his enthusiasm for the work. The former excitement he brought to each rehearsal and service was gone. His commitment to the ministry of the congregation had been replaced with deep resentment. Focusing and channeling took on a fresh urgency for Stan as he gained increased insight into the real dynamics of his own anger and his conflict with Pastor Porter:

> I've tried to talk with Ned, but he backs off so fast we hardly get started. And we need to get at some confronting. I've heard the many things he's said about me to others; I want to hear it from him. If he hates the style of music I've been doing, let him tell me. I'm fed up with his cutting me up and down the back. It's time that something be done about it, and I'm going to do it now.
>
> I know now what I want from him. I want him to report his disagreements to me directly. I want him to respect me as a fellow minister whether he agrees with me or not. I want to be able to tell him what I'm feeling about his gossiping about me to the other staff. I want to try negotiating a whole new relationship. And I want professional respect between us as fellow staff members. I recognize the validity of his anger as well as my own, and I plan to tell him so when I ask him to spell out the problem as simply as he can.
>
> I think I've focused my demands realistically. I've canceled some I know are inappropriate. I'm ready to assert the issues that are truly important to me. For all too long

I've been saying, "There's always tomorrow," while wishing that I had the courage to act today. Well, I'm waiting no longer. I'm ready to talk, and I think I can help the pastor talk too.

Two able churchmen, each capable of triggering and enhancing the other's anger, each needing to deal with his own rage and reveal his own position, but each awaiting the other's move. It is no one's *turn* to make a move; both must turn. But a turning becomes possible only where at least one of the parties has gained sufficient insight to recognize the validity of the anger and to simplify and clarify the implicit demands. Insightful focusing and channeling can lead to negotiation. Jesus' counsel is appropriate to the situation: "When another has something against you, go and be reconciled . . . When you have something against your sister or brother, go and be reconciled to the other."*

Chapter Paradigm

Recognition
　(respect the freedom to exhibit anger)
Validation
　(respect the dignity of experiencing angry arousal)
Clarification
　(respect the integrity of explicit angry demands)
Simplification
　(respect the natural, neutral, narrow, and mutual definition of demands)
Negotiation
　(cancel the inappropriate demands; confront with the appropriate; negotiate mutually satisfactory solutions)

4. The Assertive Pastor— Choosing Behaviors

Alan Brown is the senior pastor of Saint Martin's, a large downtown church with a staff of five. The focus of his current fears is Ken Whipple, his aggressive youth minister:

> The man terrifies me. When I add up all the erratic things Ken's done since joining our staff, I get paranoid worrying about what he may try to pull off next.
>
> I can't prove that he's the one who has been starting rumors about me, but in the year since he's come the number of critical stories in circulation seems to have doubled, and I'm concerned about it. When I raised the concern with him, Ken took the offensive immediately, saying that there is a lot of dissatisfaction with the leadership of the congregation. He even suggested that I listen more closely to my opposition. I was furious, but I just took it all in and then suggested we adjourn.
>
> I've listened patiently to all his past criticism of our program without batting an eye. I took his grumbling about salary—the sly digs at my income—without talking back, and I even went to the pastoral committee with his request for a raise. I've put up with a lot from Ken. If he weren't the district supervisor's son, I'd block his reappointment. But if I were to do that, everyone would know of it immediately, and the circles of conflict would only grow larger.

Alan Brown sees himself as a master of accepting criticism. He receives it with a warm, believable gentleness that disarms the critics by the time they come to their third or fourth sentence. Pastor Brown places a high value on an atmosphere of acceptance and affirmation, one that reduces tension and creates a community of peace by restraining the open ventilation of differences. He believes anger is to be controlled, concealed, and converted into a sugary mutuality.

What Alan does not see is the real effect of his nice-at-any-price strategy. An atmosphere of total acceptance and affirmation discourages others from offering genuine feedback on his ministry or daily behavior. By sacrificing candor and frankness in himself, he stifles it in others around him, so that together they live in a community of dishonesty.*

Much too genial and gentle to give level feedback to others on their behavior, he hides even from himself his own deep feelings. He inadvertently invites others around him to turn their frustrations inward against themselves, thereby generating depression, guilt, and resentment, so that together they live in a community of denial.

Far too fearful of open conflict to risk a firm confrontation, he eludes hassles and avoids angry interchanges. His associates, never sure whether their relationship could survive an emotional altercation if it did occur, are constantly on guard, so that together they live in a community of protective distancing.

Much too civilized and sophisticated to tolerate ambivalent feelings, Alan has pressed his frustrations beneath the surface of conscious awareness. Acceptant on the surface, he can remain gracious and supportive through almost any provocation. When overloaded, however, he feels—and occasionally is—explosive. His rage erupts unexpectedly, usually at home. Family members are perplexed over what mammoth explosions can be unleashed by small issues The outbursts usually come at moments when they are quite unprepared.

Nonassertive in his relationships with associates, Pastor Brown swings to aggressive ventilation when he is with his intimates. Such oscillation in conflict behavior is not uncommon.

Three Styles of Conflict Behavior

Conflict styles, when viewed from the perspectives of behavorial psychology, may be said to fall into three main groupings: nonassertive, assertive, and aggressive. To react too strongly (aggressively) or too weakly (nonassertively) is seldom effective. Between these two extremes there is a middle way (assertiveness) that is generally more useful.

Nonassertiveness

The nonassertive pastor seeks to win and sustain relationships by yielding and placating, by trying to please others, whether colleagues or competitors. In conflict situations nonassertive pastors tend to follow certain behavioral patterns: They believe the rights of others are more important than their own and deserve prior attention. They hesitate to express conflicting viewpoints, however legitimate, when there is a threat of open disagreement. In tone of voice as well as in words, they automatically placate when they fear another's attack. They are often resentful, feeling misunderstood, abused, pushed around, and exploited by others. They place themselves on trial before other persons who hold some authority position, either real or fancied. They allow the other person to shape their values and manipulate their decisions by the perceived threat of rejection. They feel forever obliged to accept additional duties, and they experience guilt after saying no to an invitation, even when they are already overworked. With impressive hindsight they frequently look back at encounters and situations, reflect on how "easy" they have been in them, and belatedly think of many things they should have said.

These nonassertive strategies can shape the whole character of a person's ministry as pacifying, absorbing, people-pleasing. The nonassertive goal of being accepted, appreciated, and affirmed by all as a "being for others" is commonly interpreted as the true expression of Christian love. It accounts for the nice-at-any-price pastor who seems to be peaceloving, all right, but whose lifestyle may actually be detrimental to true peace and real peacemaking.

A nonassertive lifestyle means a passive and superficially patient stance toward conflict. The nonassertive person believes:

"I have no power to create or demand change in an unhappy situation. I'm virtually powerless."

"I have no worth to command respect in a disrespecting relationship. I'm comparatively worthless."

"I have no rights to protest an injustice in an oppressive bind. I'm essentially helpless."

"I have no confidence in my ability to be adequate in the face of hostility. I'm incapable of withstanding threat. To confront is hopeless."

"I'm either wholly responsible or not at all responsible for the conflict. If not responsible, I must avoid it, escape it, deny it. If responsible, I must suffer openly to incur guilt."

In theological terms made famous by Paul Tillich, the nonassertive response prizes love and eschews power: "Love and power are often contrasted in such a way that love is identified with a resignation of power and power with a denial of love. Powerless love and loveless power are contrasted."* In Tillich's analysis of the extreme stances of yielding power in the name of love and discarding love in the search for power, nonassertive love may be said to sacrifice power, and with it justice. Affirming that love asks nothing for itself, nonassertiveness asks that the other respond in the same way so that each lives for the other.

Ann Fulton took over the pastorate of First Church following an authoritarian minister who had controlled everything with the power of an arched eyebrow for half a lifetime. Years of accumulated resentments had long since contaminated even the simplest communications in that congregation:

> I knew that someone was needed to draw out the poison in the congregation. As the first female to pastor them, I was the automatic target not only of those who resisted any change in pastors but also of those who resented a woman being called to the pulpit. At the same time, I was free from all the old father-figure hostility that had attended the previous minister.

Pastor Fulton could take it, she thought. And take it she did! The innuendos of multilevel sarcasm, the gossip, the silent, cold anger, the embarrassment of being ignored, the open rage of caustic criticism—she experienced it all. And she took it all in, soaked it up, without even losing her smile:

> Their pain was so great I decided mine was unimportant, so I just absorbed the negative flak. But the overload took more energy than one person could provide. I was exhausted much of the time, and resentful of my work. The zest was draining away while I listened and listened and listened to others.

Aggressiveness

The aggressive pastor is unafraid to claim and demand. Aggressive pastors often demand respect for self by ignoring others. They claim rights for self at the expense of others. They coerce, or attempt to coerce, with little regard for others.

Theologically, the aggressive response values power more than loving relationship. Loveless power exercises control at the expense of caring, although such caring is frequently distorted into a kind of caring *for* as a way of "justifiable dominance." Loveless power invades and controls. It violates others in the name of truth or righteousness or virtue.

But this power without love is ultimately worthless. Indeed, that which violates trust, love, and mutuality is itself actually powerless—unable to create lasting value. Only when power is exercised in love are wholeness, justice, and right relationships possible.*

"I saw my father get pushed around all the time by the insensitive, pigheaded people in his parish," Tim West reported, his eyes flashing. "None of that for me—I promised myself that years ago. The best defense is a strong offense. Anyone takes a crack at me, I let 'em have it. I've learned how to put people in their place but fast, with just a few well-chosen words."

Tim's aggressive solution, however, has proven to be no more effective than his father's nonassertiveness. One broken relationship after another fills Tim's emotional museum.

Sometimes the swing from nonassertiveness to aggressiveness is not an intergenerational affair. It can happen almost from moment to moment. For example, the nonassertive pastor who internalizes and accumulates frustration may in occasional periods of high stress swing all the way over to the other extreme, exploding with rage. Pastor Wills has experienced the shift: "My calling is to be a servant of God's people. I've learned to listen to another's frustration without getting anxious myself. Later though, I must admit, my stomach kills me. And my wife says I'm a real bear on Mondays. But I just take it. It's an occupational hazard of the ministry."

The aggressive lifestyle frequently alternates with the nonassertive in a common accumulation-explosion cycle. Frustration that goes unheeded gets hoarded until the tolerance level is reached, at which point the pent-up rage explodes. The ineffectual and often disastrous results of the explosion, especially when compounded by feelings of guilt from having coerced others, drives the person back even more deeply into the old pacifying and avoiding style of behavior. Once again the grievances begin to collect which will fuel the next explosion. Thus the pendulum swings from passive to aggressive and back again, but the cycle serves only to ventilate the overload while generating ever-new pressures for explosions yet to come.

The potential for such oscillation is evidenced already in the expression of certain aggressive attitudes. The ambivalence between avoidance and domination is hardly uncommon:

"I've put up with this as long as possible. Now it's time for an immediate change, and I mean to make it."

"I have no taste for power myself, but since power is the only thing some people understand, power is what I plan to use."

"I've had all I can take. I'm through with being Mr. Nice Guy."

"If I have to use force to get things changed, I'll use it."

"I have no interest in imposing on anyone, but I happen to be right. Unfortunately you're wrong. I owe it to both of us to set you straight."

"I cannot tolerate your behavior. You are to blame, not I. You are responsible for my hurt, my pain, my anger."

Because the aggressive outbursts which flow from such feelings are usually unchanneled, they serve only to heat the atmosphere, producing little of use to either sender or receiver. Being undirected toward practical ends, they succeed only in inflicting such pain that the injured person retreats in horror to the old nonassertive position. Once more frustrations accumulate until the level of tolerance is reached and all controls are blown. Thus does Pastor Wills move repeatedly from Sunday to Sunday through all the Mondays in between—as Mrs. Wills can attest!

Assertiveness

There is a constructive middle way between nonassertiveness and aggressiveness. It regards nonassertive flight and aggressive fight as equally extreme, equally futile.

The assertive lifestyle takes human worth and the dignity of human relationships seriously. Facing differences assertively, it works toward mutually satisfying resolutions. It seeks to free both sides in a conflict to prize their equal worth, respect their equal dignity, and experience their equal powerfulness.

Assertiveness as a lifestyle involves certain convictions, certain affirmations:

"I have equal worth with others. I can affirm the mutual worth of both self and others. I am worthful."

"I have equal rights with others. I will assert my wants while affirming your equal rights. I will prize justice."

"I am confident in my ability to care and to confront. I care for injuries and I confront hostilities. I can be both capable and vulnerable."

"I am responsible for my thoughts, words, and acts. I am always responsible for my behavior. I am never to blame others."

Theologically, the assertive lifestyle recognizes that loveless power violates, powerless love abdicates, but power and love in balance create justice.* Justice is the arithmetic of love that works out the fair and equal distribution of power. True power is not power *over* but power *to*. Power is the ability to be self-affirming in spite of internal tension and external negation. Power is the energy to be other-affirming as well, to live justly in equal respect for others, and to love justly in equal regard for each person's worth.

The assertive pastor respects self and others equally and asserts the rights of both self and others in an undiscourageable concern for mutual justice. Assertive pastors express the full power of their own personhood without invading the other person. They seize the courage to love without slipping into an exaggerated regard for self or for the other. Their presence represents a powerful expression of a determined love that asserts the claim of justice.

Nonassertive, assertive, aggressive—these are three ways of responding to anger and of meeting conflict situations. Each of the three styles has its own implicit set of attitudes, its own values, its own appropriate theological justifications.* Pastors need not only to be aware of them, but actually to choose between them in every instance.

Assertiveness Exercises

A person's behavioral potential, like a musician's repertoire, contains an assortment of ways for responding to frustration and threat. The more limited the repertoire, the more predictable and consistent are the person's responses. The richer the repertoire, the more flexible and resourceful the individual can be. People who have developed the capacity to recognize effective models when observing the behavior of others, and to incorporate these alternative models into their own behavioral repertoires, are more free to grow, mature, and adapt to changing situations.

Pastors particularly need to notice, evaluate, adopt, and adapt from others. They are themselves also likely to be or become models for others.

The following exercises are offered to stimulate reflection about your behavioral repertoire. Try them on for size. Think them through carefully, repeatedly. Mental rehearsal can contribute significantly to assertive growth. Your twenty-twenty hindsight can actually be put to work for you as you practice more effective responses for future interchanges.

As you read the following situations, formulate your own

immediate response. Then compare it with the six alternative responses here offered for comparison and evaluation. Identify each of these six options as being either nonassertive, assertive, or aggressive. Use them to further clarify these three major behavioral categories, but also reveal aspects of your own behavioral style and to heighten your own capacity and desire to choose among available conflict behaviors.

(1) Your salary check is late for the fourth time in a row. You are financially pressed—and embarrassed—by three major payments due the day after tomorrow, and you've already waited six days past payday without a word from the church treasurer. You dial his number, and when you get him on the phone you say: . . . .

(a) "Sam, I'm calling to ask why you're holding up my paycheck. This is the fourth time you've been delinquent. I've reported this to the finance committee. Frankly, it's time you get the system working a little better."

(b) "Sam, I'm sure you've just overlooked getting my salary check to me on time. I hate to inconvenience you. Could I drop by and pick it up?"

(c) "Sam, I'm calling to request my check before the bank closes at four today. We are a few days past the scheduled payday, so I'm hoping you can have it ready in the next four hours without inconvenience."

(d) "Sam, I'm embarrassed to be mentioning this, but I'm short financially. Could you, if it's not putting you out, get last month's check to me in the near future?"

(e) (You decide it's better just to wait a couple more days rather than stir up misunderstanding. You hang up the receiver before anyone answers at the other end.)

(f) "Sam, I'd like my check by three this afternoon.

Please have it ready for my secretary when she comes by."

(2) You get home an hour late from making hospital calls. Your wife meets you at the door. Her formal attire jolts your memory: the two of you are due at an important dinner date in a matter of minutes. Her eyes are lasers. She's biting back the angry words she had been rehearsing for the last forty minutes. You say:.....................................
....

    (*a*) "Now don't start on me about being late. For all the waiting you make me do, I've got a couple turns coming to me. So no complaints."

    (*b*) "I didn't want to go to that dinner very much anyway, and now that you're up in the air, I want to go even less. So let's forget it."

    (*c*) "Gee but I'm sorry, dear; I blew it again. I feel so rotten about my forgetting our evening schedule. I'll make it up to you some way."

    (*d*) "Just hold your tongue. So I'm a few minutes late, so what? Don't say anything you'll regret, or this will be one long evening."

    (*e*) "I'm late. I forgot all about our schedule. I can see you are angry. I would be too. Be ready in six minutes."

    (*f*) "This is the late Hal Crouse reporting in. . . . Hey, do you have to come on like your mother policing her precious schedule?"

(3) You're in a meeting with the board of elders discussing the need for an associate minister. You have already tried three times to speak up concerning staff needs, and each time Phil Holsum has cut through your comment in midsentence. Increasingly you feel irritation welling up inside. So what if he's a topnotch school administrator; does he need to play top dog to you in the board of elders? Now, at an important juncture in the meeting, you're making a crucial point when you hear

Phil knifing in again. You say:........................
....

(a) "Phil, I mean to finish my statement. If you want to try to talk above me, you'll just have to raise your voice, like you did the last three times you interrupted me."

(b) (You decide to humor Phil and just be quiet. You figure the group can make their recommendation without hearing any more from you.)

(c) (Your stomach is knotting up with frustration. You excuse yourself and leave the room. Outside, sweating profusely, you feel totally fed up.)

(d) "Phil, I'll be glad to give up the floor for your reply in just a moment. First I want to finish my point."

(e) "Phil, you've shouted me down three times already. If you're trying to make me mad, you're certainly doing it now."

(f) "I have the floor now, Phil. I'll be finished in a moment."

Tone of voice, inflection, facial expression, body postures can of course change the meaning of any response. You are probably on target, however, if you classified the various responses in these three exercises approximately as follows:

(1) nonassertive—*b, d, e*; aggressive—*a*; assertive—*c, f*.

(2) nonassertive—*c*; aggressive—*a, b, d, f*; assertive—*e*.

(3) nonassertive—*b, c*; aggressive—*a, e*; assertive—*d, f*.

Be sure to note which of the responses most closely resembles your own and what that suggests about your own style in the matter of conflict behavior. Recognizing that you can choose, run through the exercises again to see if you can move away from the unproductive extremes and toward constructive assertiveness. Formulate some exercises of your own, growing out of your own most recent experiences with frustration and anger. Rehearse the new response you'd like to try when and if such situations should recur.

Chapter Paradigm

Powerless love
Plays impotent
In nonassertive
Evasion.

Loveless power
Plays omnipotent
In aggressive
Invasion.

Loving power,
Powerful love,
In assertive
Affirmation.

Love with power,
Power in love,
Is justice.

5. The Modeling Pastor— Inviting Assertiveness

Charlotte is chairing the meeting. Her "come let us play os-trich" speech seems to be carrying the day with the board of elders: "The only way to avoid a split in the church is to look the other way until this charismatic excitement dies down. If we just ignore the charismatics, give them no attention at all, they'll lose their appeal. Let them have their little meetings; we'll get on with business as usual."

Warren Green struggles to contain the impulse to interrupt. Pastor Green is confident that ignoring the conflict, as Char-lotte suggests, can only increase misunderstanding and heighten distrust. He is about to speak up when Mark Schmidt, a junior high math teacher, breaks the silence: "If we ignore a group with as much visibility as the charismatic fellowship, that can only mean rejection to them. I have decided that I will neither reject these people nor allow myself to be rejected by them. I'm going to keep my friendships alive with them. I'll even be sitting in on some of their meetings. I will not let myself be walled out."

Pastor Green watches with delight as Mark's old nonasser-tiveness drops away. Mark used to shrink from confrontation. Lately he's been giving up old habits of passive avoidance and trying new ways of coping with tense situations. When dif-ferences arise at the school where he teaches, Mark has re-cently been striving to act more positively. Now he's obviously applying his new learnings to a larger conflict. The pastor senses that perhaps his own assertive model has begun to catch on—at least with Mark. And if it can catch on with one per-son, then hopefully there will be another, and another, and . . .

The Pastor as Model

The styles of communicating, confronting, asserting, and affirming used by a congregation's leadership tend to reappear quickly in others, not only in the staff around them but also in the congregation and even in the wider community. We all tend to do what we have seen others do often and well.

The ability freely, reflectively, and purposefully to choose one's way of responding is a necessity for effective ministry. It can be cultivated by investing time in reflection on how we react to others and by consciously seeking to respond by choice rather than chance. The more capable we are in learning from others' models and the more able we are in making selected models our own, the more rapidly can growth, maturation, and effective conflict management be achieved. The ability to learn from observation as well as from the trial and error of participation is what frees humans to make long strides in changing self-defeating anger styles into positive, community-building anger. Pastors especially need to learn from models, for whether we know it or not we do a great deal of modeling ourselves.

If in a tense moment of conflict a pastor responds firmly and caringly, those who observe can learn to do the same. They learn it by watching the actual exercise of anger in love and by noting its consequences. To learn is to discover that something new is possible. That learning is especially effective when we see the new possibility realized in and by someone we trust. Modeling can often be the major gift pastors give to their people. Sermons may fade with little recall. Counseling can be filtered to admit only those facets that reinforce what the counselee wants to hear. But the modeling that pastors do is unavoidable, unforgettable, and hard to distort to the viewer's own bias or ends. Such modeling can bring love and power together in redemptive ways.

Affirmation and Assertion

Action that is at once both positive and powerful is unfamiliar behavior to most persons. We are more familiar with action that is characterized by either one or the other but not both of these qualities. Indeed, to act powerfully by asserting strength and to act positively by affirming respect for relationship are two separable styles that are commonly available to most persons. But to see both exercised simultaneously in balanced integrity is so uncommon that for many it is thought to be altogether contradictory.

To be assertive (act powerfully), however, does not require any loss in affirmativeness (act positively). Nor does an increase in affirmativeness necessarily decrease one's power in being assertive. Care for relationships (affirmative action) and concern for goals (assertive action) are coequal components of effective response to others.* Effective pastoral care involves both. It embodies clean assertion and clear affirmation. Together they express both love and power in their redeeming juxtaposition.

Assertive-Affirmative Anger

Assertive anger focuses its demands clearly and acts firmly, whether in changing one's own behavior or in requesting appropriate change from another. Such clean, clear anger is an art to be learned.

Affirmative anger is an even more crucial skill to be mastered. Anger that acknowledges the equal worth both of myself and of you is focused on the barriers between us rather than on the faults we see in each other.

Destructive, nonaffirmative anger attacks persons. It erects barriers and creates distance. It commonly takes the form of blaming and cutting criticism: "You are an insensitive lout." "You're coldly critical and intolerant." "I am totally fed up with you and your blaming." Notice the labeling, the blaming, the rejection and withdrawal.

Affirmative anger, on the contrary, attacks the situation between us. It cuts through the tension and confusion, levels the accumulating misunderstandings between the parties, and seeks to reduce the distance and distrust: "I am angry about the misunderstandings that keep on accumulating between us." "I want this cycle of irritation and frustration out of the way." "I miss the times when we're close and everything is open between us." Note the focus on the issues between us, the frustrations separating us, the old anger cycles entrapping us, the valuing of the relationship.*

Assertive-affirmative anger unites power with love. It recognizes that affirming is primary and asserting is secondary in ongoing relationships, but that both are essential if the relationship is to prosper. As pastors develop skills both in prizing persons and in valuing mature personhood, a balanced model can begin to emerge in our ministry style.

Assertive-Affirmative Balance

Assertiveness means having something to stand *for*. Affirmativeness means having someone to stand *with*. Effective assertiveness is grounded in authentic affirmativeness. The two need to be brought together in appropriate fashion. The pastor who models an appropriate assertive-affirmative balance will be able to stand *for* human values while standing *with* the humans valued. The balance will show up in a variety of ways:

TRUSTING/RISKING

There is a balance, a relationship of interdependence, between ability to trust and willingness to risk. Indeed, trust and risk go hand in hand in human relationships. As trust increases, new risks can be taken. Each additional risk taken represents both an extension of the trust experienced and an invitation to the expression of greater trust. So risk follows trusting, while trust springs from risking.

Risk is grounded in trust. To risk more than our shared trust warrants is to live dangerously.† I trust you to be able to hear my anger without feeling blamed or rejected. That trust allows me to risk owning the anger I feel and sharing it with you: "I imagine you can see how upset I am about being stood up today. I don't need to hide my anger with you. Nor do I need to hesitate telling you what I want from you in the future—OK?" Such risking is hardly conceivable without trust, but such risking almost certainly builds trust as well.

LOVING/LEVELING

Love is the opening of the self to another. Leveling is the open sharing of that self in all its dimensions. Open loving and openly leveling are intimately, indeed integrally, related. The two may be distinguished but hardly separated. They go hand in hand.

The kindest and most loving thing I can offer you is the truth. When I love you, I share with you my perceptions, values, beliefs, and feelings—my self. But I am loving only if as I offer "my" truth I am equally open to hearing and receiving yours. I not only love to level; I love your leveling as well.

Loving you enough to be genuinely angry about the obstacles in our relationship is what enables me to express my feelings without fear that such expression will destroy our friendship: "I really am for you, and I'll stand with you no matter what. But that doesn't mean I agree with what you're doing to yourself. I'm furious at the way you keep punishing yourself for being something less than perfect." Such leveling presupposes love, and enhances it.

CARING/CONFRONTING

A balance needs to be struck between caring for your needs and confronting the issues between us. Indeed, the two go hand in hand. Whoever cares confronts. Whoever does not confront does not care. Confronting is grounded in care. When a firm base of caring exists, differences can be hassled, frustrations aired, and mutually satisfactory solutions sought.

Caring for another is not just an attitude of appreciating, understanding, and feeling with another. Such attitudes, when inappropriately lavished on a person, can be very uncaring in their effect. Caring means bidding others to grow, to realize what they truly are and are becoming. I affirm my respect for you as you are while at the same time declaring my expectation that you be all you really are:* "Our relationship really does matter to me, and I'm showing how much it matters by telling you how deeply I disagree with your decision to separate from Sherri without first at least meeting with a counselor." That kind of confrontation is really a declaration of care.

EMPATHY/INSIGHT

The insight I would offer you must be balanced by a sensitivity to what you are actually experiencing. Empathy and insight are needed in equal measure. Understanding must precede interpretation. I need your support as much as your criticism. The empathic pastor stands *with* others before offering them insight.*

Anger which is expressed in a context of empathic valuing can affirm acceptance of the person even as specific behaviors are called in question. Critical insight is useful in the context of an expression of firm support that can increase another's sense of well-being. When I offer criticism primarily to "get a load off my chest," it is seldom of much use. Blend criticism with support: "I appreciate your frustration with my lateness; I'm frustrated about it too." "I do not appreciate your complaining about me to others rather than reporting the problem directly to me." Critical insight needs to be—and be perceived to be—offered in the context of empathic support.

Community-Affirming Assertiveness

The pastoral care of anger is concerned with more than one-dimensional assertiveness. Self-assertion can often be an exercise in self-serving individualism. Assertive models that focus on *my* rights while ignoring yours may offer immediate reduction of tension but without long-term enhancement of relationships. Any use of power that violates another cannot truly vitalize the self. Any act that is unjust to another injures the actor. Effective assertiveness accordingly involves a community focus.

Self-assertion training is useful in pastoral counseling—not as an end, however, but as a means. It is not a goal in itself but a method to free persons from passivity and conformity. Its purpose is to build the individual—not at the expense of the community, however, but with a view to community building as well.

A self-realizing assertiveness may well be useful for the individual who is so absorbed by the community as automatically to comply with all its expectations. Focused assertiveness can help free such persons from a binding atmosphere of conformity and obligation. But to learn and practice self-assertiveness is to utilize only one pole of the ellipse of wholeness. The other pole has to do with the other person. Self-assertion and affirmation of others are both needed. To assert power without at the same time affirming a balanced respect for other persons can further their alienation. It can also compound my guilt; it can create a boomerang effect whereby I am absorbed back into a dependent relationship involving loss of self.

A community-affirming assertiveness is thus concerned with more than simply the nonassertive/assertive/aggressive power dimension; it is equally concerned with the nonaffirmative/affirmative/absorbing love dimension. A pastoral model of assertive-affirmative behavior seeks a balance in both dimensions: assertiveness rather than the extremes of nonassertiveness or aggressiveness, plus affirmation rather than the extremes of nonaffirmation or absorption. Centered love (affirmation) and centered power (assertiveness) must complement each other in the wholeness of powerful loving. The model can be diagramed to highlight these two dimensions.

Human beings do not live unto themselves. We are always inevitably involved with others. The diagram, whose two axes focus the two dimensions of our concern for both assertiveness and affirmation in dealing with anger, also serves to highlight four areas of our concern for the human relationships that are at stake. It suggests the importance of an equal measure of freedom, responsibility, respect, and regard in our relationships with one another.

Rights

We each have equal rights in our relationship. We each have the freedom to say yes and no; the freedom to think,

A Two-dimensional Model of Love and Power

Equal Rights

We each have equal freedom:
to feel, to act, to choose;

to be rightfully angry,
to be rightly loving.

(I will not evade you
in anger or anxiety.)

Equal Respect

We are each of equal worth:
to value self and other;

to respect worth when angry,
to protect worth when loving.

(I will not invade you
in love or hate.)

NONASSERTING   ASSERTING   AGGRESSING

NONAFFIRMING AFFIRMING

ABSORBING

Equal Responsibility

We have equal responsibility:
to affirm love,
    assert power,

to exercise the ability of anger
    response,
to experience the ability of
love response.

(I will not avoid you
in fleeing relationship
or fighting community.)

Equal Regard

We can hold each in equal
    regard:
to love with equality,
    live in mutuality;

to be angry at our alienation,
to be loving in our affirmation.

(I will not void the
meaning of your presence
in community and creation.)

feel, and act as an autonomous self; and the freedom to be the initiator, evaluator, and administrator of our own decisions. These rights are to be equally prized, equally exercised, equally enjoyed.

We are equally free to take the consequences for our own acts, and to work out misunderstandings, misbehavior, and injustice in redemptive ways. We have equal rights to the past.

We are equally free to be spontaneous, to trust hunches, to be illogical, to be flexible. We have equal rights to the present.

We are equally free to choose, to change, to grow. We have equal rights to the future.

Responsibility

We each have equal responsibility in our relationship. My thoughts, feelings, judgments, words, and acts are wholly mine; for them I am fully responsible. Your thoughts, feelings, values, words, and acts are solely yours; for them I am in no way responsible.

I will not be responsible *for* you (I will not play God). I will not be responsible *to* you (I will not make you my god). But I will be responsible *with* you in loving and leveling, in caring and confronting.

Respect

We are each of equal worth. We each deserve equal respect as persons who are of irreducible value, worthy of being loved simply because we are we.

We are worthful as we are, not as we act. Ours is a created value, not an earned value.

I will not see you as inferior to me. Neither will I see you as superior to me. You are a worthful you, and I am a worthy I.

Regard

We can each hold the other in equal regard. This is the real genius of love.

The biblical notion of agape is best understood as equal regard. When agape is viewed as benevolence it becomes paternalistic; condescension is the worm in the apple of Christian charity. When seen as self-sacrifice, agape can ultimately be self-righteous. But when understood as equal regard, agape prizes both self and other as equally precious, equally worthful, and irreducibly valuable.*

Equal rights, equal responsibility, equal respect, and equal regard—these are the four sides of authentic humanness and effective relationship. These are the product where assertiveness and affirmation come together in appropriate balance, where centered power and centered love are redeemingly juxtaposed.

When my rights oppress your rights, freedom is betrayed. When my responsibility either evades or invades your areas of responsibility, justice and integrity are impaired. When I do not respect you equally with myself, dignity and worth are denigrated. When I regard myself as "more equal"—even "less equal"—than others, agape is violated.

Pastors need not fear to appreciate and use assertiveness in their care and counseling. Affirmative assertiveness is community building in both intention and effect.

Assertive-Affirmative Modeling

The pastor, associate pastor, Christian education director, and youth minister are sitting around a table in the church library. The atmosphere of the staff meeting is tense, as if an unspoken conspiracy of silence has grown thick and impenetrable in recent weeks. Ted Horning, the youth minister, finally breaks the tension: "I don't see how we can go on without discussing the Bill Williams scandal; after all, that's the topic of discussion in all the other groups in the congregation." An almost audible sigh of relief goes around the circle. At last the issue is out on the table.

Bill Williams, the congregational chairperson, is the subject of a spicy rumor being circulated throughout the community.

As the story has it, Bill has been sexually involved, apparently for some time, with his executive assistant, Vickie. Three years ago Bill's wife, Marge, was paralyzed following pelvic surgery for cancerous tumors. She has been confined to a wheelchair ever since, and sexual relationships are impossible. Vickie has become almost a member of their family. Now, when Marge's cancer is recurring, although almost no one knows of its recurrence, the rumor is afloat that Bill is "on the make" elsewhere—and virtually everyone knows that!

"Frankly, I'm wondering if you've been covering for him, Pastor." Ted looks down at the floor, afraid to make eye contact with Pastor Felici. "Bill has made some mighty big financial contributions—it's hard to bite the hand that feeds you, right?"

The pastor's anger is immediate and intense. (So Bill is wealthy, so his real estate business has turned a handsome profit, so a lot of people are jealous of his success; is this any reason for Ted to be fingering himself righteously? Is adultery more evil than covetousness?)

Ted struggles to contain the momentum within his indictments. He bites back the sarcastic words about to shatter the minister's silence: "Just because philandering Bill could buy out the congregation with his pocket cash is no reason to wink at his sexual escapades."

Pastor Felici withdraws as the conflict threatens to escalate. The whole team follows suit.

Long-standing frustration in congregation and staff had mounted to the point where the most likely member had finally lost control and moved to aggressive attack. The pastor was unable to respond. Ted was unable to control. No one was able to move in the direction of a redemptive solution.

Ted's position embraced several points of view: (1) Vickie is a warm and exciting person; since she and Bill are together much of the time, the rumors obviously have a base of truth; (2) Bill's wealth is power, and he's bought out the pastor; (3) someone will need to call a rake a rake; (4) anger is the only possible response to such goings on.

The pastor's withdrawal is no match for such a situation. There is pain here that must be faced with affirmation, and there is anger here too that must be confronted with assertiveness if any resolution is to result.

Stop for a moment. Reflect on what response you would make if you were the pastor. Then compare your imagined response with some of the options Pastor Felici might conceivably have employed:

(1) "I notice that the rumor is never told without a reference to Bill's wealth. Makes me wonder if people are concerned about his morals or his money, whether their problem is another person's lust or their own greed" (passive-aggressive response).

(2) "Our primary concern has to be for the congregation and its future. If Bill's reputation is in public question, perhaps we should ask him to resign his chair until everything clears up" (nonassertive avoidance of working through).

(3) "If we have any human concern, we've got to stand by Bill. His wife is terminally ill; he and Vickie are Marge's support system. These are the people who are in the most pain. Their hurt comes first" (all-affirmative response).

(4) "I suggest that we discuss it no further until one of us talks to Bill, Marge, and Vickie. Whether the rumor is true or is not true, they'll need someone to stand with them now. And they deserve to hear what's going on. I'd like to be one who talks with them. Shall we go together, Ted?" (asserting and affirming simultaneously).

Pastoral ministry is enriched when assertive and affirmative responses to anger are effectively conjoined. Where the pastor adopts that style and models it well, the whole atmosphere of the congregation can change. Traditional patterns of denial are broken or at least reexamined. Passive wait-and-see attitudes are challenged. Hidden aggression is called out into the open where it can be scrutinized. The congregation is helped to face anger and even confrontation.

Pastors who want to introduce a new way of expressing hostility must risk modeling it even though their efforts may initially be misunderstood. Assertive action, however affirming, is often perceived as a threat by those who see it for the first time, but gradually they will begin to understand. People who observe affirmative assertiveness done effectively come to see it as an alternate behavioral model, and even to feel: "I can do that too; that could work for me just as well, maybe even better."

Revising Expectations

When people observe a new model of conflict behavior, or experience it at first hand as participants in the actual altercation, they begin gradually to understand it. In time they may even identify with it and assimilate the new response into their own repertoire. One of the first fruits of such experience, whether by participation or observation, is the revision of expectations. An expectation is an estimate of probability held by the individual that a particular reward will follow a specific behavior in a given situation. People who thought they knew exactly what would happen discover that things can turn out quite differently.

Every behavior routinely carries with it a full set of expectations. We tend to take for granted the probable effects of every act. We assume its impact on relationships. These expectations are all estimates of the probability that a particular outcome will occur:*

"If I am kind, gentle, and forgiving to others, they will automatically be the same with me."

"If I conceal my anger and act pleasingly nice, you will control your frustration and be equally nice."

"If I yield immediately and selflessly before your anger, you will feel guilty and then defer to me."

"If I come on strong and threatening with my anger, others will usually yield to me to play safe."

"If I admit my weakness and vulnerability, I will be pounced on and scorned."

Anger expectations are a strange and mixed bag of hopes and fears. They need constant examination and correction.

Unexamined and uncorrected, they can immobilize a person with anxiety even before the anger is recognized.

Frequently our anger expectations are nothing but unretouched photographs of our parents' anger and the consequences it usually produced. The behaviors we most resented when we were children are often the very ones we ourselves reproduce when as adults we find ourselves in threatening situations.

As an adult, however, I must reconsider the expectations learned in earlier stages of growth and anticipate new outcomes for old behaviors. Models learned long ago must be challenged, reworked, and reconstructed.*

To that end old expectations must be first confronted. Pastor Wilson is trying to help John Hardy do just that:

"Pastor, I can't tell my dad that I don't want to be a doctor; he'd kill me barehanded."

"Tell me about how you'll make it through medical school, John, when your heart is in becoming a sculptor."

"I'll just flunk out of college; that should take care of his high hopes for my brilliant success. Of course that's asking to be annihilated too."

"Let me hear how you would go about breaking the news to him that you're planning a career in art."

"I said I can't tell him." (John's expectations are totally catastrophic, being rooted in his boyhood memory of his parents' divorce and an older sister's rebellion and exclusion from the family.)

Pastor Wilson then does a role play to heighten John's awareness and to foster critical evaluation. The pastor plays an assertive son who is confronting his dad and who is doing so with equal firmness and affirmativeness. "Won't work," says John flatly. The model as such is appropriate, but it is not useful or believable until John's expectations have been tested and restructured. So the pastor plays the role of father and has John test out his ability to be both fair and firm, caring and confrontive, toward the older man. John responds well to the challenge. He gets more and more assertive.

Finally he breaks into laughter. In the process the old expectations dissipate and John begins to formulate new anticipations about the possible outcomes of behaving strongly.

Expectations are the rewards anticipated; reinforcements are the rewards one actually gets. Quite apart from the senior Mr. Hardy's response, John's new assertiveness is its own reward as he feels the new power that is present within him. As John comes on affirmatively, the new respect he finds in relationships and the new sense of justice he experiences in conflict situations assure the permanence of his new styles. The reinforcements, though not always calculable, do compare favorably with John's enhanced expectations.

Expectations can of course take the form of prophecies, especially where they presage defeat: "I'm going to try talking to my dad, Pastor—I can't do any more than fail."

But the wise counselor will not let the matter rest there. "Yes," the pastor replies, "it is possible that you won't get what you want on the first try. But I doubt if that will devastate you, John, because whatever his response you'll be proud to have expressed yourself forthrightly already on the first round. Success can come later."

A new anger-expressing behavior, even if it's more constructive, seldom wins immediate rewards the first time around, at least externally. Except for the positive reinforcements inside—the delight one feels in acting powerfully, purposefully, with integrated caring and confronting—the anger may receive only negative rewards until in due time it earns respect. This is why rehearsing expectancies and outcomes should embrace more than one round. Restructuring a relationship takes time. Extended rehearsing can lengthen a person's expectations to include rounds two, three, and even four of the anticipated conflict.

Short-range expectations demand immediate results: "I want this change to happen as soon as possible, preferably yesterday." Anger often expresses itself that way. Even with rehearsal it may convert old feelings of impotence into fantasies of omnipotence that demand instant blind obedience from the other. For this reason rehearsal of expectations needs to cultivate the longer perspective. "I want a change as soon as possible" articulates my anger while respecting the other's time frames. Long-term expectations must be built into the new models as they are rehearsed beforehand, repeated afterward, and reaffirmed daily. When others register surprise at my new assertiveness, when they feel anxiety at being called to respond in unaccustomed ways, I need not feel discouraged. Indeed, even that response is a signal to me that change is occurring. Their resistance would not be evoked if my style was not taking a new turn. When old expectations are called in question and new expectations entertained, growth begins to occur.

Facilitating Behavioral Growth

There are ways in which the pastor can help others to move concretely toward growth in dealing with anger. Specific steps can be taken within the counseling process to assist individuals in considering, trying, and adopting new responses:

(1) Discuss together and arrive at a tentative hypothesis concerning which anger responses need changing. Mutually specify and clarify what the individual is doing that isn't getting the desired results.

Clients who are critical of the other person's behaviors and have little ability for assessing and criticizing their own may well behave toward the pastoral counselor as toward any other person. A disrespectful son will treat the counselor with disrespect. A woman who comes with a plunging neckline and a dress so tight that her appendectomy stitches show through is exhibiting in the counseling setting her basic approach for getting attention in other situations as well. The alert pastor welcomes such carryover from the noncounseling context because it allows for meaningful observations of behavioral patterns yet to be focused and articulated.

(2) Get samples of the actual behavior *behind* the reper-

toire of responses the individual is using. Help the individual to see the connection between precipitating behavior and response and between response and ensuing outcome.

A wife says, "My husband treats me terribly." "What does he do?" "He hits me." (After I club him with a frying pan.)

A youth says, "I have lousy parents." "What behavior brings out the louse in them?"

A wife says, "I've a lousy husband." What is she getting out of living with such a guy? Some need is being fulfilled, or people wouldn't endure pain or seek to rescue a loser.

It may take patience and repeated effort to help people see the realities and establish the connection. The effort will require empathy and can lead to insight.

(3) Define the payoff anticipated from each behavior now used in time of conflict. Expectations need to be seen and understood before they can be revised.

What is there inside of me that leads me to expect a certain outcome if I choose response A over response B? What in fact do I expect of each response? My expectations were learned in childhood and youth. They seemed to work well then, at least sometimes, but now they seldom work. The pastor can help people examine their expectations and even contemplate alternative payoffs. New responses are needed to win new rewards!

(4) Model new alternatives. Role play new options. Experience new responses. Attend to how they are rewarded.

If all I do is attempt to eliminate an old and ineffective response without finding, trying, and adopting a promising alternative, I am no better off. When stress arises, confusion will follow, and the old response will return with a vengeance.

A thoughtful human can articulate and even demonstrate behavioral options in words, but role playing can do more. It not only gives insight into behavior, but also shows a better way of behaving. Educated neurotics may be able to trace their behavior quite knowledgeably to their mother but then keep on repeating the self-defeating response, almost as if the knowledge itself were reinforcing it. A negative behavior will not disappear as long as it continues to gain rewards. When the new behavior doesn't produce immediate results, the person naturally falls back on the old, and since the old is familiar, it continues. Simple insight into how self-defeating the old behavior is may sometimes actually increase its occurrence unless the better option is rewarded and the old option goes unrewarded. A person who talks of suicide often gets reinforcement from the listening-hearing-supporting that ensues; so additional action may be necessary. Involving the person in a group, gradually reducing the counselor's undivided attention, and rewarding new behaviors are often useful techniques in this connection.

Caring people so easily get drawn into giving rewards for the wrong thing. "What is the behavior, and what is its payoff?" Those questions need to be asked constantly, and precise answers sought.

The easy, well-modulated, sweet, lovable souls will easily win reinforcement for their niceness. But that may be what's messing up their lives. So let them experiment in a role where they get tramped on and discover how useless niceness can be. For the first time in their lives, let them see that niceness does not always get the expected rewards. Then model new ways of coping, reward the new behaviors, and watch the number of possible responses increase.

Three crucial aspects of setting up roles can be mentioned here: (*a*) sense the person's expectation and assign a role which will frustrate it, giving negative rewards for the use of old behaviors; (*b*) model a new response, elicit whatever internal or intrinsic rewards the situation calls for, and offer your own external reinforcement; (*c*) encourage persons to try on the model, to fill it out with their own perceptions, values, and goals, and to compare results.

(5) Encourage the taking of risks. Help people to take risks in trying on a new behavioral style at home, at work, or in the company of friends. Practice of a new style in a group counseling situation can reduce fear and increase choices in the other situations of life.

The pastor must be willing to put people in roles which will hurt, not in order to be mean or nasty or see people suffer, but because they've asked for an opportunity to grow. All therapy is relearning. If the learning situation is kept as close as possible to real life, there will be greater possibility for transfer to life situations. Role play can be done with real, live, breathing persons. Such authenticity can bring out authentic feelings.

It is not artificial for the pastor to enter into a role play with a client. Such a technique can constitute a slice of real life, bringing two real people together, albeit in a nonthreatening setting. In the safety of the counseling situation, new behaviors can be tried on, new responses tried out. "Trying" is appropriate in behavioral rehearsal in order that some comfort with the alternate style may be achieved in advance. Such advance testing can assure that the assertive-affirmative model, when implemented, is a matter of integrated experience rather than of merely random intention.

Living and Modeling

Modeling is most effective when it happens naturally, spontaneously, almost accidentally. To act assertively and affirmatively because that is the nature of maturity and the nexus of ministry is the goal of a pastor's continuing personal and professional growth.

The models which have taught me most were those I observed when the other was unaware or had completely forgotten that I was watching. The best models are those that are simply being their own authentic selves. When one is "speaking truth in love" or "embodying grace and truth"— Paul and John both have such expressions for balance—then wholeness becomes visible, believable, and utterly contagious.*

Chapter Paradigm

Anger in love, loving anger,
Asserts the power of being,
Affirms the value of relating

with equal respect
for our equal rights
in equal responsibility
as the equal regard of agape.

Living and loving powerfully—
The model is contagious.

6. The Effective Pastor—Releasing Congregational Anger Creatively

"Pastor Jameson, I suggest that you offer your resignation—immediately."

Tony Cordova avoids meeting the pastor's eyes. Having delivered his ultimatum, he fishes out his car keys and fingers them idly. As far as Tony is concerned, he's finished as chairperson of the board; he's ready to exit after recommending the same for the pastor.

Pastor Ron Jameson's first year as minister of Holy Trinity is almost over. The honeymoon period is ending more abruptly than he could ever have imagined. The safe wall of denial that made these first months so hassle-free was finally fractured. Tony's ploy encouraging the minister to look for a call to another church is typical of Holy Trinity; it is a characteristic attempt to quiet an emerging conflict before it can spread or even be heard beyond the board.

Pastor Jameson is in a state of shock. He's not receiving a call, but he is hearing voices: "So I got angry tonight at a board member for gossiping about the associate pastor's wife. How could one confrontation with the church board produce such an instant impasse? I might have known that no congregation could be as perfect, as acceptant, as forgiving as this one claimed to be. . . . I guess I should have considered some other career: plumbing or forestry or janitorial services."

An intuition that had haunted Ron since coming to Holy Trinity was now an obvious reality: although few waves of anger ever break the surface calm of this church, this peaceful community has within it several accumulated generations of mighty anger deposits deep down, as on an ocean floor; these subterranean currents are so immensely powerful as to be terrifyingly destructive if they ever surface. And now it has happened. Ron's sneaking suspicion has become solid insight.

The Anger-Accumulating Community

An all-loving, anger-free community can only be an illusion. At times it is even an intricately complex delusion constructed and maintained by a united community front: "No differences here; no disagreements allowed." The delusion necessitates a deep commitment to peace-keeping even at the cost of individual and group integrity. The commitment to peace at any price is on the side of denial and distortion. An easy peace of surface niceness, avoidance, and unawareness is on the side of pretense and even pathology. It creates delusions.

"They were such a warm and friendly group when I first interviewed the congregation," Ron Jameson recalls. "When I asked how differences were managed at Holy Trinity, they only smiled. Then someone commented, 'We don't have any really major differences. Things work out in time.' I obviously walked into this with my eyes closed. I too was caught in the contagion of denial. I refused to see what was; I chose to see only what I wanted to see. I set myself up for disappointment. Then I started pushing, too hard and too fast."

At the moment, Pastor Jameson wishes he'd taken a longer look at Holy Cross, the other congregation which had approached him about the same time he chose Holy Trinity. But Ron had read in the initial letter from Holy Cross: "We've experienced a good deal of open conflict in the past five years. We've come to expect it as a normal part of our living and working together. If these words sound foreign to you, you may not find us attractive . . ."

"Sounds like they're high on hassling," he'd said jokingly. The joke had eased his anxious feelings a bit. But by the time he'd answered their letter, his fears of an open-with-conflict group had eliminated that congregation from consideration.

True, open conflict and unconcealed anger can be a danger sign when it is chronic, cyclical, and monotonously confined to unchanging factions within the congregation. But open conflict that is progressive rather than repetitious, purposeful rather than simply a matter of discharging tension, and innovative in the sense of dividing and redividing the group along constantly changing boundary lines can be highly creative. Such creative conflict can indeed cause a congregation to be "high on hassling," although they are likely to call it by many other names: negotiating needs, discussing differences, debating disagreements, or working through the difficulties of life together in community.*

Congregations that handle conflict creatively are not typical. More often than not, churches are unaware of the anger accumulating within, an anger that often appears unpredictable, confusing, even puzzling.

Puzzle 1: Serious divergences may stalemate into a steady state of contained anger, while incidental differences erupt into open hostilities. For example, Christians for two thousand years have affirmed the teachings of One whose life and death epitomized nonviolence, while at the same time they have initiated the most violent wars in human history. The very churches that have managed for centuries to live with this weighty war-versus-peace paradox have often suffered massive and bitter schisms over fine points of theological debate.

Puzzle 2: Some conflictual anger quickly runs a natural course to some adequate resolution, while other conflicts tend to escalate, permeate additional areas of community life, and resist all attempts at channeling. For example, anger and resentments between the Smiths and the Joneses about the competition between their children—who dates whom, and who wins in athletics and academics—will likely run a natural course to resolution as the young people themselves mature. But an endemic conflict between two extended family systems that have been feuding for generations and vying for dominance in the same congregation can outlast the best attempts at resolution; in such a situation pastors may come and go, but the congregational turmoil can simmer on for generations.

Puzzle 3: Anger irritation may be decreased by the high mobility of group members (the natural turnover attendant upon moving and transfer into and out of a community), while anger may be increased through the surface abrasiveness of new people involved in short-term relationships where group trust remains low. Oren Felcher, an oldtimer at Saint Mark's, was glad to have the new factory move in at the far end of town, but as far as his church was concerned: "I don't know those new people. Sure I'll fight them if they try to muscle in." Contrast, however, the feelings of Abe Mason in a changeless, old mountain church: "I've known all the folks in this church for as long as I can remember, and I can't stand them. I reckon I do get a kick out of turning the place inside out!"

Pastors can help people at least face the puzzling phenomenon even if they cannot always resolve the issue. Congregations accumulate anger as surely as individuals do. Accumulated anger can be frightening and even devastating in its expression.

Attending to the Anger Inducers

Effective pastoral care will seek to reduce the accumulation of anger in a congregation. It will endeavor to identify those irritants within the community that consistently produce frustration, and then diminish their presence as far as is feasible. There are several anger inducers that particularly bear watching in this connection.

Indifference

Indifference elicits anger. When a community ignores the individual or familial pain of its members, it thereby inhibits the discharge of frustration, and anger tends to accumulate. Unless there are built-in safety valves to drain off hostile sentiments, the system will overload and anger irritations will accelerate. The pastor often serves as a safety valve for human pain, allowing angry parishioners to release hostility in a safe setting by shifting it from the original target onto the minister. Displacement is the technical term for such a shift: the expression of emotion is switched over onto a substitute target that can take it, but not take it personally. Pastors able to understand and allow such displacement can often open the whole system until it provides many listeners who will hear the human hurts of others and facilitate their healing.

Where there are no channels for venting hostility, no opportunities for expressing dissent, the emotions nonetheless linger and fester. People unhealed will eventually be heard.

Closed systems arouse authority problems in participants who feel chronically ignored or invalidated. Open systems welcome continuous input and feedback from all members. In a congregation where people can suggest themes for studies, elective classes, growth groups, sermons, and retreats, their personal investment reduces the fantasy of an authority system that is indifferent to their needs and insensitive to their contributions.

The Christian community is by definition an open system functioning, bodylike, in every-member integration. To be alive to all the body and alert to all its needs is both means and end of the Christian community functioning as an organism.

The pastor who provides low-threat occasions for the expression of disagreement and discussion of differences is continually discharging the static or irritation. Talk-back sessions for dialogue on the sermons can release the resistance generated by listening to what is either intended or perceived as superego-oriented preaching. Periodic evaluation sessions that invite negative as well as positive feedback can neutralize some of the hostilities generated by the system or projected onto the system from other sources.

In this whole area there is much room for experimentation, but little room for indifference. Pastors who ignore anger accumulation in the congregation are missing an opportunity for significant ministry to individuals and to the community.

Inferiority

Inferiority induces anger. Inferiority theories of anger have a long history and illuminate one of the key anger processes.

The process runs something like this: inferiority induces anxiety, which in turn produces obsessions, which in turn elicit anger.

A situation occurs in which my appearance, performance, or behavior is viewed as less acceptable than somebody else's. The feelings of inferiority attendant upon this frustrating situation generate anxiety within me that throws me emotionally out of balance. The anxiety floods my awareness with obsessive thoughts of self-justification or recrimination as ways to regain equilibrium. The fantasies of superiority and fears of inferiority trigger angry blaming, attacking, or even martyring behaviors that are designed to restore my sagging self-esteem.*

Anger, viewed as a response to inferiority feelings, functions as a natural, normal, homeostatic response to emotional imbalance. A lowering of mind appraisal stimulates a heightening of body arousal. As surely as hunger rises when blood sugar drops, so we become hostile and fantasize about retaliation when we experience disrespect and when self-esteem is decreased.

Hostility can be reduced in persons and relationships as social inferiority, which is its source, is overcome. Systems that live by vertical models of superiority/inferiority, power/ powerlessness, haves/have-nots, oppressed/oppressors of course stimulate such hostility. The liberating community is at war with such violent systems. Male-female injustice and racial-social-political discrimination, exploitation, and domination are all dehumanizing. Where inferiority is reinforced, hostility is generated. Where equality is experienced, conciliation occurs.

Inferiority feelings are the specialty of many congregations in which self-worth is depressed by a rich assortment of strategies. A no-self-worth or low-self-worth theology may reward persons for denigrating their self-esteem; persons convinced of their own worthlessness—frequently, they believe, in accord with the golden rule—inevitably see others as equally worthless. Similarly, communities which place a premium on success, performance, appearance, achievement, wealth, or intellect can exaggerate unfriendly comparisons and stimulate inferiority feelings.

The liberating community, by contrast, is a leveling community. It reduces the occasions for inferiority/superiority comparisons. It fosters equality of self-worth. Pastoral care seeks to reduce hostility. It facilitates mutuality and a communal experience of the agape which means equal regard.

Impotence

Impotence brings on anger. When persons feel powerless, when situations appear hopeless, when change seems impossible, hostility results.* Frequently the anger is turned inward: the feelings of helplessness and hopelessness generate depression and loss of mastery. Turned outward, however, such impotence can evoke rage.

Pastoral care of persons in a state of emotional depression or in socially oppressive situations and economically depressed conditions must welcome the awareness and expression of anger and provide settings for its open acceptance, clarification, and conciliation. Expressions of indignation must be prized as necessary motivation for human liberation. Deeply embedded grief that is not processed for release and healing can stimulate within the system an impotent rage that can only intensify and spread.

Harold Gruver, a veteran pastor with a good track record in managing previous conflicts, was suddenly inundated with waves of hostility from the congregation during his fifth year of ministry at Saint Philip's. The anger of the parish was focused not only on him, but also on his wife. Mediators called in from outside the congregation were at a loss to discover either the dynamics or the purposes of the conflict. The situation grew worse until the pastor's resignation was finally demanded and given.

Especially puzzling to Pastor Gruver was the strange configuration of people ranged against him. Many were persons who had received much pastoral care from him during their times of crisis and had in fact been solid supporters of his ministry for years. Continued reflection at last suggested a common denominator: during the three years preceding, virtually all his attackers had experienced severe grief as a result of personal loss. The congregation had lived through a remarkable series of tragedies: automobile accidents, airplane crashes, and drownings as well as cancer and coronary deaths. Furthermore, the community's grieving style was dominantly one of denial. There was a high demand for persons to be brave, believing that God makes no mistakes and that all things happen according to his purposes. The anger that could not be expressed to such an arbitrary deity was later released on God's local representative.

Unable at the moment to recognize that the group was laying all this pain at the minister's doorstep, both pastor and people tried to deal with the hostility as if it involved merely a personality hassle, an interpersonal failure, or a theological disagreement. What had actually happened, though, was that as personal anger was added to the community pain, it was multiplied by misplaced analysis and further compounded by incriminations.

Pastors can develop an awareness of residual pain. They can sense the buildup of anger in the congregation. And they can be particularly alert to the need for care and counseling to deal with such anger in situations of indifference, inferiority, and impotence. Pastoral care can often limit the scope and effects of anger accumulation in the congregation.

Anger and the Congregation

Congregations can be characterized—and frequently are characterized—in terms reflective of their respective approaches to dealing with anger. Pastors have long known about the frozen community, the healing community, the creative community. But pastors also need to consider the role of ministry in the origins of such typology and the ensuing categorization of churches. Indeed, the aware and insightful pastor who personally models assertiveness can effectively move a congregation into new and creative ways of changing its approach and style in this regard.

The Frozen Community

Cornell Sadler had always regarded Morningside Church as a low-conflict community. Events there overtook him by surprise. Pastor Sadler reflects on how the tensions developed:

> I excused myself from the board of deacons meeting early to be with a family whose father had just died of a massive stroke. Minutes after I left, a motion demanding my resignation was made by a man whose family I had supported through a similar crisis, as well as through three other major losses in recent years. The motion did not carry, but the airing of tensions and of dissatisfactions with my work that began in the meeting that night quickly spread and continued in many forums for weeks to follow.
>
> Over the next three months I deliberately looked the other way and simply doubled my efforts at pastoral work. That approach didn't seem very fruitful. Slowly but surely, much that I had helped to build—community, solidarity, team spirit—began to fall away. Five years of careful work were gone in ten weeks.
>
> If I had called for a vote of confidence somewhere along the way, I'm sure I could have won it easily. But knowing how the older people of our congregation had experienced church fights of long ago as incurable trauma, I did not want to bring the present conflict to an open rupture just to keep myself in office.
>
> Eventually trust eroded between me and the leaders of the church boards. The rest of the congregation was largely detached from the problem because of their uninvolvement in the church's decision-making process. I felt that the only way out was for me to resign. The people that came to the board meeting where I announced my decision were four to one in favor of my staying, but I thought it best to protect the church from further conflict and therefore refused to reconsider. I even declined to accept more than six months' severance salary.
>
> Sadly enough, in the year that followed, a large number of people left the church anyway, including the moderator, the finance chairperson, four elders and their families, and the six strongest families in the young adult group. I still don't understand it—the very thing I tried to prevent hap-

pened anyway. I don't know how I could have worked any harder than I did to keep things together in a peaceful way. I don't know what more I could have done.

The denying community slowly collects pain, frustration, resentment, and anger until the tension becomes intolerable. With no channels open for horizontal release and healing relationships, the stress converts to some appropriate form of hostility, often against an authority figure. Pastor Sadler's approach was to internalize and absorb the tension. Morningside tended to follow suit: matching his model, the community turned pain inward as well. Unable to deal with anger, it became a frozen community, inflexible, unadaptable, hostile.

When hostility is contained rather than expressed, it eventually emerges in a playing out of old scripts: unfinished authority hassles, unresolved parental tangles, and unmanageable dilemmas of rebellion against God. The pastor easily becomes the common screen for a whole audience of parishioners projecting onto the minister the silent films of their own emotional museums. But there are alternatives to the frozen community.

The Healing Community

When feelings are prized and shared, emotional ice fields may begin to thaw. Tensions which may have been greater than the community's loyalties could channel can be released in ways that actually draw people together, as in a magnetic field of warm acceptance. Those who share suffering are knit together at a deep level of genuine sympathy. They have met each other in a way that is profoundly bonding. When hostility is allowed to surface in an atmosphere of caring and support, the hostility-generating community can become a healing community.

As persons discover the delight of community, fears of indifference and rejection can be dispelled. People actually hunger for acceptance, and with all that hunger around there's little reason for people to starve if they can find each other: Those who mourn receive comfort. Those who rage receive understanding. Those who fear receive reassurance. Those who are suspicious learn to trust. Those who are oppressed can receive justice. Hostility, where it is openly expressed and shared, can cut through indifference and call compassion into being.

As failures, losses, and personal tragedies are shared, persons gather around in support, and the anger expressed becomes grief shared. Fantasies of crushing inferiority can be dispersed. Real injustices can be corrected. Hostility appropriately vented in a context of acceptance can even help to renegotiate and restore relationships, building equal respect.

As the sense of weakness is shared, courage emerges from the mutual concern. The frustrations of crippling impotence are dissipated. Vulnerability becomes a new kind of strength. Hostility, where it is worked through, releases power.

Real compassion in community emerges from pain healed, hostility heard, grief released. Compassion derives from the experience of community; it also deepens community as numbness is converted to sensitivity, anger to affection, and hostility to healing.

Community humanizes us. When human suffering, pain, or anger comes to us through a real person—someone who can be seen, named, touched, embraced—it is humanized, and healing is present to be claimed.

We can be open to experience the anguish of others' suffering. We do that when we are willing to live with the helpless recognition that we can do nothing to save them from their pain—except to stand alongside, hearing the hurt, validating the anger, sharpening the demands, and being human together. In healing, sadness speaks to sadness, anger cries to anger, worth affirms worth, forgiveness evokes forgiveness, and grace calls to grace. All these can be received; none can be given. To be real, they must be claimed by the receiver.

The crucial factor for healing in community is deep human encounter. As we make our own faith and doubt, hope and despair, anger and tenderness available to our sisters and brothers, we touch each other at the core of life, and healing happens. Anger attends pain, but pastors can work to assure that it becomes therapeutic rather than numbing.

The Creative Community

Real community occurs where conflict and concord flow freely back and forth in a continuous rhythm, each growing out of and giving way to the other in dynamic reciprocity. Community involves a rich sequence: concord, followed by conflict, that leads to concord, that turns to conflict, and on and on. In every state of peace the conditions of future conflict lie embedded. In every conflict the potential of a more transcending peace awaits fruition.

Creative community grows where free conversation occurs. A congregation is a true community only as it is truthful in inviting its members to feel freely and speak revealingly their inmost feelings, hopes, and values. Community means the integrating of people's diverse perceptions in a rhythm of unity and discord that produces wholeness and balance. For a congregation to seek unity without discord is to deprive its members of wholeness; they possess only such wholeness as remains when all that causes discord drops away. The more successfully such a congregation can implement its strategies of denial, the more impoverished is its community and each of its participants. When both unity and discord are prized, however, the group's whole experience of its energies and tensions can enrich the people's joint discoveries of humanness and transcendence.

True community involves a matrix of both friends and enemies where all alike are needed, valued, and incorporated. All are valued as a source of learning. All are experienced as warp and woof of the fabric of life together. In true community even the opponent, the antagonist, is prized. I need my enemy to keep me vital, alive, alert. Criticism and opposition, pressuring and provoking are indispensable to my growth. I love my enemies by challenging their creativity in return, by strengthening their viewpoints in response, by bolstering their arguments in dialogue. As enemies we bid each other grow; so even in our enmity we function as friends, seeking each other's fulfillment.

The creative community delights in our wholeness as persons and in our fullness as the new persons we are called to become through life in the Spirit. The community of the Spirit is a new humanity where humanness is not lost but released to grow into vital integration. The congregation can be such a creative community.

As human beings we are created for community. As members of the congregation we are recreated in and through our life in the community of the Spirit. Creative pastors can play a vital role in the creative, Spirit-filled community as they become aware of their own energies and personally model ways of channeling anger that are assertive and affirmative, thereby freeing their congregations for a similar caring and creative style of healing and release.

Chapter Paradigm

End illusion,
Speak the truth;
Be the truth,
Each with the other,
For we are members
One of another.

Let your anger
Be without alienation.
Do not contain it,
Deny it, or distort it
Into destructive rage.

Be caring;
Be a forgiving community,
As God has modeled in Christ.
Live in love.

—Ephesians 4:25–26,
31–32; 5:1–2

Notes

Page

ix. * Leonard Berkowitz, "The Case for Bottling Up Rage," *Psy-*
`ology Today, July 1973, pp. 24–31.
3. * Eph. 4:25–32; Col. 3:5–17; Gal. 5:16–25.
4. * Frederick Perls, Ralph Heferline, and Paul Goodman, *Gestalt*
Therapy (New York: Bantam Books, 1974).
6. * For a careful treatment of these controls as defense mechanisms,
see Anna Freud, *The Ego and Mechanisms of Defense* (New
York: International Universities Press, 1946).
7. * George Bach and Herb Goldberg, *Creative Aggression* (New
York: Avon Books, 1974), pp. 23–24.
13. * Stanley Schachter, "How Emotions Are Labeled," *Psychologi-*
cal Review 69 (1962): 225.
14 * Frederick Perls, *In and Out of the Garbage Pail* (New York:
Bantam Books, 1969), pp. 171–72.
15. * Schachter, "Emotions," pp. 231–32.
17. * Perls, Heferline, and Goodman, *Gestalt,* section 1.
18. * Theodore Isaac Rubin, *The Angry Book* (New York: P. F.
Collier, 1969).
19. * This is an adaption of Perls' treatment of owning projection,
attribution, retroflection, and introjection. See Frederick Perls,
Gestalt Therapy Verbatim (New York: Bantam Books, 1973).
23. * Murray Bowen, "The Use of Family Theory in Clinical Practice," *Comprehensive Psychiatry* 7 (1966): 345–74.
25. * Kim Giffen and Bobby Patton Gitten, *Basic Readings in Inter-*
personal Communication (New York: Harper & Row, 1971).
26. * Jack Gibbs, "Defensive Communication," *Journal of Com-*
munication 2 (1961): 141–48.
36. * Jay Hall, *How To Interpret Your Conflict Management Survey*
(Conroe: Teleometrics International, n.d.).
37. * Matt. 5:23–24; 18:15–18.
39. * Bach, *Aggression,* pp. 23–24.
41. * Robert Alberti and Michael Emmons, *Your Perfect Right* (San
Luis Obispo, Calif.: Impact Press, 1974).
42. * Paul Tillich, *Love, Power and Justice* (New York: Oxford University Press, 1954), p. 13.
44. * Ibid., pp. 39–40.
45. * Ibid., pp. 67–68.

Page

52. * Hall, *Conflict Management Survey,* pp. 4–7.
53. * Rollo May, *Power and Innocence* (New York: W. W. Norton & Co., 1972).
53. † Giffen and Giffen, in *Basic Readings.*
54. * Milton Mayeroff, *On Caring* (New York: Harper & Row, 1973).
55. * Charles Traux and Robert Carkhuff, *Toward Effective Counseling and Psychotherapy* (Chicago: Aldine Publishing Co., 1967).
59. * Gene Outka, *Agape: An Ethical Analysis* (New Haven: Yale University Press. 1973).
62. * Sharon Bower and Gordon Bower, *Asserting Yourself* (Reading, Mass.: Addison-Wesley Publishing Co., 1976).
63. * Albert Bandura, *Aggression: A Social Psychological Analysis* (New York: McGraw-Hill, 1962).
68. * Eph. 4:15–16; John 1:14, 17.
72. * Lewis Cozer, *Functions of Social Conflict* (New York: Free Press, 1962).
75. * Milton Layden, *Escaping the Hostility Trap* (Englewood Cliffs, N.J.: Prentice-Hall, 1977), pp. 5–15.
76. * My treatment of impotence and rage and their interrelationships within community is indebted to May, *Power and Innocence.*

Annotated Bibliography

Alberti, Robert, and Emmons, Michael. *Your Perfect Right.* San Luis Obispo, Calif.: Impact Press, 1974.
————. *Stand Up, Speak Out, Talk Back.* New York: Pocket Books, 1975. Two outstanding books on assertively claiming your own rights in interpersonal conflict situations. They provide clear outlines for understanding the crucial differences between assertiveness and aggression.

Augsburger, David. *The Love-Fight: Caring Enough to Confront.* Scottdale, Pa.: Herald Press, 1973. A popularly written guide to effective caring and confronting relationships in marriage, family, work, and community situations. Blends psychology and theology for a creative Christian expression of wholeness in personhood.

Bach, George, and Goldberg, Herb. *Creative Aggression.* New York: Avon Books, 1974. A psychoanalytically oriented book on assertiveness and the ritualization of aggression in intimate relationships.

Bower, Sharon, and Bower, Gordon. *Asserting Yourself: A Practical Guide for Positive Change.* Reading, Mass.: Addison-Wesley, 1976 An explicit training workbook on behavioral rehearsal and assertive thinking, negotiating, and contracting.

Bry, Adelaide. *How To Get Angry without Feeling Guilty.* New York: Signet Books, 1976. A self-help book that attempts to define types of anger and anger behavior with a view to bringing anger under the control of insight and responsibility.

Fensterhelm, Herbert, and Baer, Jean. *Don't Say Yes When You Want To Say No.* Nem York: David McKay Co., 1975. A helpful and easy-reading book on assertiveness in widely varied situations with many scripts and scenarios for practicing new behaviors.

Fromm, Eric. *The Anatomy of Human Destructiveness.* Greenwich: Fawcett Books, 1973. An inquiry into the nature of human aggression from a psychoanalytic perspective.

Layden, Milton. *Escaping the Hostility Trap.* Englewood Cliffs, N.J.: Prentice-Hall, 1977. A popular approach to eliminating hostility in interpersonal relations by reducing inferiority feelings and raising self-esteem.

Lazarus, Arnold, and Fay, Allen. *I Can If I Want To.* New York: William Morrow & Co., 1975. An excellent book that describes how a number of irrational myths can keep people from acting assertively. Brief, concise, effective in outlining ways to go about changing self-defeating thoughts and behavior.

May, Rollo. *Power and Innocence.* New York: W. W. Norton & Co., 1972. An existential psychological approach to understanding the nature of human aggression, power, and hostility. A significant viewpoint for pastoral care.

Mayeroff, Milton. *On Caring.* New York: Harper & Row, 1973. The best available book on caring and on the nature of loving relationships which free people to both give and receive support and affection in rewarding relationships.

Nye, Robert. *Conflict Among Humans.* New York: Springer Publishing Co., 1973. One of the best textbook surveys of the behavioral and social psychological research on conflict and negotiation in human relations.

Phelps, Stanlee, and Austin, Nancy. *The Assertive Woman.* San Luis Obispo, Calif.: Impact Press, 1975. A highly useful training book for assertiveness as a woman in a society that has reinforced nonassertive behavior for females.

Rubin, Theodore Isaac. *The Angry Book.* New York: P. F. Collier, 1969. A highly readable book on anger and its distortions by an outstanding author and psychiatrist in the psychoanalytic tradition of Karen Horney.

Shriffrin, Nancy. *Anger, How To Use It.* Canoga Park, Calif.: Major Books, 1976. A guidebook to various anger therapies from the various streams of psychological theory and therapeutic approaches.

Smith, Manuel. *When I Say No, I Feel Guilty.* New York: Bantam Books, 1975. A creative, funny, and at times outrageous method for outmanipulating manipulators by use of assertiveness. High on asserting. Low on affirming.

Southard, Samuel. *Anger in Love.* Philadelphia: Westminster Press, 1973. A psychoanalytically oriented pastoral approach to anger, marriage conflict, counseling, and pastoral therapy.

Tillich, Paul. *Love, Power and Justice.* New York: Oxford University Press, 1954. A brief classic treatment of the nature of love, power, and their balanced integrity in justice.

Wahlroos, Sven. *Family Communication.* New York: Signet Books, 1974. Twenty rules to improve communications and make your relationships more loving, supportive, and enriching for emotional health in the family.